Zachary Taylor

12th President of
the United States

A veteran of 40 years in active military service, General Zachary Taylor had little knowledge of politics when he became the 12th President of the United States in 1849. (Library of Congress.)

Zachary Taylor
12th President of the United States

David R. Collins

 GARRETT EDUCATIONAL CORPORATION

Cover: *Official presidential portrait of Zachary Taylor by Joseph H. Bush.* (Copyrighted by the White House Historical Association; photograph by the National Geographic Society.)

1999 Printing

Library of Congress Cataloging in Publication Data

Collins, David R.
    Zachary Taylor, 12th president of the United States.

    (Presidents of the United States)
    Bibliography: p.
    Includes index.
    Summary: Traces the childhood, education, employment, political career, and presidency of the man nicknamed "Old Rough and Ready."
    1. Taylor, Zachary, 1784–1850—Juvenile literature.   2. Presidents—United States—Biography—Juvenile literature.   [1. Taylor, Zachary, 1784–1850.   2. Presidents.] I. Title.   II. Title: Zachary Taylor, twelfth president of the United States.   III. Series.
E422.C65   1989   973.6'3'0924—dc19   [B]   [92]
88-24539
ISBN 0-944483-17-8

Contents

Chronology for Zachary Taylor

1784   Born on November 24 in Orange County, Virginia; grew up near Louisville, Kentucky

1808   Appointed a first lieutenant in the 7th Infantry of the U.S. Army

1810   Married Margaret (Peggy) Smith on June 21; promoted to captain

1812   Received brevet rank of major for gallantry in action

1815   Resigned Army commission

1816   Reinstated as a major in the U.S. Army

1819   Promoted to lieutenant colonel

1832   Promoted to colonel

1838   Brevetted to brigadier general after defeating the Seminoles at the Battle of Lake Okeechobee

1846–1847   Brevetted to major general; won recognition for military leadership in Mexican-American War

1848   Elected 12th President of the United States

1849   Resigned from the United States Army

1850   Died on July 9

Chapter 1

Washington Heat

Summer came early to Washington, D.C., in the year 1850, and it came without mercy or kindness. Dust hung in the air, occasionally shifting direction with the movement of a passing carriage. Landscapes, usually cloaked in rich green grasses, lay parched and worn while the thirsty Potomac River slithered like a slender snake beneath a scorching sky. Blistering and relentless in its determined quest to torture those mortals who would challenge its fury, the sun reigned as king.

"It would not surprise me if someone did not blame this Devil's heat upon me," a disgruntled President Zachary Taylor remarked to one of his aides. "It would seem that everything else worthy of complaint has been hurled in my direction."

Indeed, the observation made by the 65-year-old chief executive seemed appropriate. During the 16 months Taylor had occupied the White House, one accusation of wrongdoing after another had found its way to his door. Often, so very often, he missed the military life—a world in which sides were clearly drawn and where careful planning, shrewd strategy, and bold maneuvering made the difference between victory and defeat. There was a challenge in that world, goals worth seeking, rewards to the winner. Within the world of politics, however, the rules were so different. In fact, Zachary Taylor barely understood the rules at all.

It was not entirely Taylor's fault. A man who had served 40 years in the military – constantly moving, never staying long enough in one place to even qualify as a voter – could not be expected to have intimate knowledge of the ways of the nation's capital and the delicate machinery of government. He had been too busy fighting Indians and Mexicans, too involved with building and defending forts. Politics was a full-time task, one which demanded attention and care.

Taylor often chuckled to himself when he recalled the letter sent by the Whig Party notifying him of his nomination as its candidate for the presidency. He was in Baton Rouge, Louisiana, when the letter arrived "collect." Taylor refused to accept it, as he refused to accept any unpaid mail. There were many times in the 16 months he had been President when he regretted *ever* accepting the word of his nomination.

As naive as Taylor was about politics and the presidency when he became 12th President of the United States, he was fully aware of why he had been selected as the Whig candidate. He was a war hero, pure and simple, and war heroes made attractive candidates. He was the fourth person to make his way to the White House after commanding men in battle. George Washington had been the first; Andrew Jackson, the second; and William Henry Harrison, the third.

As a plantation owner in Virginia, Washington had combined his soldiering with a deep interest in civil government. Jackson had served in the U.S. Senate before becoming President. Harrison, too, had served in Congress before his presidency.

Taylor, however, was still an active major general in the U.S. Army when approached about running for the nation's highest office. Lacking any political experience whatsoever, his first inclination was to turn down the Whig request and retire gracefully with his beloved wife, Peggy, to their river cottage in Baton Rouge. But the lure of the presidency had proved too attractive to a man who had enjoyed the reins of leadership for so long. Now he found himself caught in a quagmire of doubts and confusion.

PAUSE FOR CELEBRATION

For the moment, Zachary Taylor wanted to forget his political troubles. He would not allow anything to dampen his spirits as the people of Washington, D.C., prepared to celebrate the Fourth of July. Few Americans were more patriotic than Zachary Taylor. And as this particular Fourth of July approached, he was especially excited because the holiday festivities would include dedication of the Washington Monument cornerstone. Certainly there seemed no more fitting observance for the holiday than those activities that would honor the noble Washington, the man known as "the father of his country." If only the sun would hide itself for but a few hours, long enough to spare the crowds from its intense heat.

Under a Blazing Sun

Zachary Taylor arrived at the monument site early. Wearing appropriate formal attire for the occasion, he immediately felt uncomfortable. The heat of Mexico and Florida had often been terrible, but this Washington sun was intolerable. Yet tolerate it Taylor did, sitting in the open, bright glare and listening to one speech after another. Taylor sipped ice water constantly, now and then resting the cold glass against his sweat-covered cheeks.

By the time the three-hour program ended, the President complained of feeling slightly dizzy, even giddy. He happily returned to the coolness of the White House, where he began eating a large basket of fresh cherries. He accompanied the cherries with a half dozen goblets of iced milk. An aide suggested a short nap before dinner, but Taylor would have none of it. He was still hungry and guests were expected for the evening meal. Taylor changed clothes and prepared to act as host.

One of the dinner guests was the White House physician, Dr. Witherspoon, who could not hide his shock at Taylor's weary appearance. The doctor was dismayed that the President had spent such an exhausting day in the fiery afternoon sun. After the meal, Taylor continued to treat himself to more cherries. Witherspoon felt compelled to warn him of the potential dangers of such consumption after such a long day in the heat. But Taylor, more inclined to give orders than take them, continued to feast. A short time later, however, he began to complain of stomach cramps, and Witherspoon insisted the President take to his bed.

Another Battle to Fight

As hours became days, the stomach pains persisted, joined by headaches and fever. Rumors in Washington ranged from "He's recovering beautifully" to "He is in his final hours." Action in Congress slowed as leaders sought the latest news about the President's condition.

Behind the doors of the White House, family members gathered to care for their beloved patriarch. A thin, plainly dressed Peggy Taylor tended her husband in the presidential home, just as she had in Army outposts for 40 years. She was totally confident of his recovery from the stomach disorder that kept him in bed.

As news circulated through the nation's capital and beyond that the President was ill, perhaps fighting for his life, people gathered to share stories and pray. There were so many soldiers with whom Taylor had served, so many tales of "Old Rough and Ready," a military leader who had no use for fancy uniforms and formal ceremony. Zachary Taylor was a common man, a man born to the people, born when the nation itself was still in its infancy.

Chapter 2

On the Kentucky Frontier

W hen Zachary Taylor was born on November 24, 1784, in Orange County, Virginia, the country's 2,400,000 people were scattered over 13 states that were bound together by a loose alliance, the Articles of Confederation. Zachary's father, Colonel Richard Taylor, had won acclaim as a soldier during the Revolutionary War battles of White Plains, Monmouth, and Brandywine. As a reward for his military efforts, Colonel Taylor was given 6,000 acres of land in Kentucky. He decided to claim his war bonus seven months after Zachary was born. When Baby Zach, his two older brothers, and his parents moved to Muddy Fork, Kentucky, they were helped by the family's six slaves, usually referred to as "field hands" in genteel society.

The Taylor homestead, located about six miles northeast of Louisville, Kentucky, rested on the edge of undeveloped frontier land. A one-room log cabin that Colonel Taylor constructed upon the family's arrival in Kentucky was soon replaced by an impressive plantation home that the family called Springfield. Colonel Taylor quickly established a reputation in the territory for his honesty and hard work. He was a justice of the peace and soon became a customs collector at the port of Louisville, assessing taxes on incoming goods. He helped write the laws when Kentucky was granted state-

Zachary Taylor was born on November 24, 1784, in this austere, sturdy home in Orange County, Virginia. He was the third son of Colonel Richard Taylor and his wife Sarah. (Library of Congress.)

hood in 1792, and also served in the state legislature. Convinced that the local frontier was safe from wild animals and blood-thirsty Indians, Taylor and his wife Sarah added to their family, until it finally included seven sons and two daughters. One of the sons, Richard, died in infancy.

BUCKSKIN BOY

There was much to do for a boy growing up in the Kentucky frontier. Young Zach, named after a deceased grandfather, loved the outdoor world, his skin forever sunburned in the summer and ruddy from winter winds. His thick, muscular frame was most often clothed in buckskin, blue jeans, moccasins, and a coonskin cap. It was an outfit shared by many boys in the territory, largely to imitate and emulate the area's hero in residence, Daniel Boone, who made frequent local appearances to the delight of his fans.

Springfield came to be a center of socializing among family, friends, and neighbors. Zach welcomed his friends to his home, and although their rough-housing antics occasionally drew a nonapproving grimace from Sarah Taylor, there was a general tone of harmony and hospitality always present. As the passing years added to the family wealth, Colonel Taylor bought additional surrounding acres and planted more tobacco and hemp. "You can always get a good cigar and the finest goblet of wine at the Taylor place," area visitors were told, and the generous colonel and his wife never failed to make good on those words.

Getting an Education

Having received good educations themselves, both Colonel Taylor and his wife were determined that their children would be equally well-schooled. After doing their own tutoring for a while, the Taylors joined with other residents in hiring Elisha Ayer from Connecticut to provide the local children with a more systematic, disciplined education.

Ayer was instrumental in securing the services of Lew Wetzel, a legendary frontiersman, who offered the students lessons in how to survive in the wilderness. Zach took a special interest in learning how Wetzel handled a musket and knife, becoming one of the quickest members of the class in loading the firearm and accurately hurling a mounted blade.

Somewhat later, Zach was sent to an academy in Louisville. Although he never acquired polished skills in spelling and writing, Zach could, nonetheless, convey his thoughts with purpose and force, an ability that would prove useful in later life. Reading was more to Zach's liking. He could not get enough of adventure stories and tales of military heroes and their battles. His personal admiration for his father and the older man's willingness to share endless Revolutionary War experiences no doubt fanned Zach's early interest in soldiering.

PROMOTING THE PUBLIC GOOD

Colonel Taylor made no conscious effort to instill within his children the importance of public service, yet the lesson was passed along by his example. "My father gave us few speeches about our obligations to promote the public good," Taylor recorded later, "but we were constantly aware of the affairs of our community. In addition, we were dutifully made aware of the Taylor family motto –'Ready and Faithful'– and we stood ever waiting to put the words and thoughts into practice."

Zach was a frequent visitor to nearby Louisville, which continued to grow because of its position along the Ohio River. He enjoyed talking to residents as well as to those who were just passing through town. "You're a people person," his father remarked often, and Zach sensed the words were offered as a compliment.

Young Zach was a favorite among the field hands at Springfield, largely because he was not above swinging an ax, plowing a field, or helping to harvest a crop. As a son of the plantation owner, he could have avoided such tasks. But if there was a job to be done, Zach would find it. The thought that he was in any way different from or above the workers of the land did not occur to him. He was especially willing to help build a new neighbor's house or barn when another family moved into the area and would encourage his mother to invite any newcomers for a meal.

A YOUNG SOLDIER DREAMS

The 400 acres immediately surrounding the house at Springfield were dubbed "The Home Place"; as a young man, Zachary Taylor took a special interest in their upkeep. Bushes and shrubs were carefully manicured, particularly in the areas near the wide driveway circling the house. And because Colonel Taylor never forgot the importance of being able to view an approaching enemy, he insisted that those lawns close to the house be kept clear. Zack took these orders as his own, always hoping to please his father.

Young Zach also prided himself on being a light sleeper, always ready to spring into action at a moment's notice. There was not much need for such alertness, but Colonel Taylor's war stories often referred to the importance of an early warning in case of a surprise attack. Zach felt especially privileged to occupy a bedroom on the second floor that was directly opposite his parents' room. He took as an unassigned responsibility their safekeeping for the night.

War games and military strategy were a constant part of Zach's freetime thinking. Colonel Taylor encouraged his son's fondness for the military life, but Mrs. Taylor did not share her husband's enthusiasm. "I shall be happy to know that your skill with a musket will be confined to shooting an occasional deer or grouse for dinner," she told Zach more than once.

Despite a deep respect for his mother's wishes, Zach found it impossible to squelch his growing interest in an Army career. William, an older brother, was a second lieutenant in the artillery. Although he achieved little distinction while in the Army, William was a strong spokesman on behalf of military service. He shared with Zach stories of new friends, of adventurous training sessions, of being ready to take on any possible challenge that might come along.

A Dream Realized

As Zachary Taylor slipped comfortably into his 20s, war clouds began to appear on the American horizon. After President Thomas Jefferson's acquisition of the Louisiana Territory in 1803, Spain periodically would raise a fuss about the boundary line between American land and Spanish-controlled Mexico. Diplomatic relations were no better with Great Britain. Pockets of bitterness over the outcome of the Revolutionary War still lingered among many American residents who had remained loyal to England, and frontiersmen pushing westward encountered resistance from numerous Indian tribes still loyal to the British. Moreover, the British had been harassing American ships on the high seas for several years. The most serious incident occurred in June 1807, when the British frigate *Leopard* stopped the U.S. frigate *Chesapeake* in American waters. The captain of the *Leopard* demanded the right to board and search the *Chesapeake* for British deserters. When the captain of the *Chesapeake* refused to comply, the British fired on the American ship, killing three sailors and wounding 18. They also boarded the ship and took four men as British deserters. The action caused President Jefferson to triple the size of the American Army, from 3,000 to 9,000 men, and a new regiment, the Seventh, was also authorized.

Zachary Taylor was ready. It was time to stop playing soldier and start being one. Without hesitation, he requested assignment to the new regiment. His was one of many such applications, but he had the backing of the Kentucky delegation in Congress. And it was no handicap being related to James Madison, who was then Jefferson's secretary of state. On May 3, 1808, Secretary of War Dearborn, acting on behalf of President Jefferson, officially named Zachary Taylor a first lieutenant in the Seventh Infantry. It was a month before the new officer was notified. He then responded with strong enthusiasm but weak spelling and grammar:

> Louisville, Ky., June 6th, 1808
>
> Sir,
>
> I received your letter of the 4th of May in which you informed me that I was appointed a firs Lieutenant in the seventh regiment of Infantry in the services of the United States which appointment I doo accept.
>
> I am Sir with great respect
>
> > your Obt. Servt
> > Zachary Taylor
>
> The Honrl H. Dearborn S. at War

Thus it was that the 23-year-old Virginia-born, Kentucky-raised Zachary Taylor began a military career that would entail his total dedication for the next 40 years. Never could he have known the adventures that lay ahead. Perhaps it was better that he did not.

Chapter 3

Attack on Fort Harrison

Z achary Taylor's appointment as a first lieutenant in the United States Infantry was overshadowed by news of the death of his older brother William in late June of 1808. Indians had attacked Fort Pickering, killing William and a number of other soldiers. To the eager and enthusiastic young Taylor, it seemed appropriate that he would be going into the Army as a family representative. But the thought had little appeal to his mother, who, while grieving one son, was having to say goodbye to another.

It might have soothed Sarah Taylor somewhat had young Zachary sought admission to the U.S. Military Academy at West Point, which had opened in 1802. There, he would have received several years of technical and practical military training before engaging in any combat. But Zachary had little desire for such formal preparation. He felt that the skills he had acquired on the Kentucky frontier would serve his purposes adequately. He could scout, hunt, and shoot better than most men, and as for managing men, he had assumed much responsibility managing the slaves at Springfield. Yes, Zachary Taylor felt ready and able to plunge into action. But as the summer of 1808 came to an end, the new first lieutenant still had not received any orders.

GATHERING RECRUITS

Finally, in September, Zachary was told to report to Captain Hord in Washington, Kentucky, to assist with getting recruits for the new regiment. Traveling by horseback, Taylor arrived in the small town in northeastern Mason County only to discover that his commanding officer was sick in bed. Having secured just a drum and fife player for the regiment but not a single recruit, Hord immediately placed the recruiting duties in his new lieutenant's inexperienced hands.

Recognizing there were few young men in Washington interested in joining the military, Taylor requested that the recruiting offices be moved. Hord agreed, and Taylor moved the recruiting headquarters a few miles east to Maysville, which was strategically located on the Ohio River. He hoped to entice into the Army both the men who traveled the waterway and those who roamed the backwoods. It was a wise plan or, as called in military language, a "strategic maneuver," which the new, young first lieutenant would continue to perform throughout his military career.

By the following spring, Taylor had successfully recruited two companies of soldiers. But he was tired of the paperwork and longed for an opportunity for military action. Thus, he was delighted when he and his recruits were ordered to join the rest of the Seventh Infantry in New Orleans, Louisiana.

DEADLY DUTIES

After enduring one of the coldest winters on record in northeastern Kentucky, Taylor and his newly arrived recruits found themselves sweltering in New Orleans' blistering heat. To make matters worse, General James Wilkinson, the officer in charge, chose to station his troops some 13 miles outside the city, in a mosquito-infested swamp. Wilkinson, a veteran of the Revolutionary War, worked his soldiers constantly, drilling them or having them building improved fortifications. Moreover, the food supply was insufficient and often contaminated, making the men easy prey for infection.

After yellow fever broke out, the tired and weak soldiers had to spend much of their time burying their fallen comrades. Seeing what the future could easily hold, some men stole off in the night, choosing desertion over what they considered a worse fate.

First Lieutenant Zachary Taylor also became a victim of the fever. As his once stout frame wasted away, his legs could hardly support the weight of his body. Only a year before he had entered the service with the hope of an impressive military career. Now it appeared that he would die before ever being in a single battle. However, orders for a furlough arrived, offering the weak and depressed Taylor an opportunity to return to Springfield for a much-needed rest. His father welcomed him home with a soldier's salute, which young Taylor returned before collapsing in his parents' arms.

Road to Recovery

Never before had Zachary so appreciated the luxuries of hot food, clean water, and a soft bed. Not only did the bedrest give him a chance to recuperate, it also gave him ample opportunity to read and analyze every book or paper about military strategy that he could find. Such information was to prove useful in the years to come.

As soon as he could, however, Taylor was again exploring the family properties, hunting and fishing, and visiting with anyone who had the time. The color returned to his cheeks, the strength to his body. Before long, he was riding into Louisville to enjoy the social life of the community.

At the age of 25, Zachary Taylor married Margaret Mackall Smith, his beloved "Peggy," on June 21, 1810. (Library of Congress.)

It was at a dinner party in Louisville that Zachary Taylor first met Miss Margaret Mackall Smith, called Peggy by her friends. Dark-haired and slender, this exciting young belle from Maryland clearly reflected an education obtained both in the United States and Europe. Yet there was no arrogance, no flaunting of her wealth and position.

Never before had Taylor been so impressed by a woman. He immediately began calling upon the enchanting Miss

Smith, making little effort to hide his marital intentions. His feelings were obviously shared, for on June 21, 1810, the couple were married at the Taylor plantation. Zachary was 25; his bride, 21.

For a wedding gift, Colonel Taylor gave the newlyweds 324 acres of land at the mouth of Beargrass Creek. As soon as he was strong enough, Zachary began building a home with the help of slaves and neighbors. In the years to follow, Peggy Taylor would return to this home to have five of the couple's six children.

New Orders

Before the house was completed, Zachary received orders to rejoin his regiment. It was not easy to leave his new wife and an unfinished home. But Zachary Taylor was a soldier, and military orders took priority over anything else.

Following instructions, Taylor rode south to return to his regiment, only to find there was no official assignment for him when he arrived. Having nothing to do, he quickly returned home. Then, in November 1810, he received notice that he had been promoted to the rank of captain. This action left Taylor scratching his head, considering the amount of limited service he had performed as a soldier. "One cannot always understand how such things happen," Colonel Taylor told his son. "You merely accept the fact that it does."

When the new Captain Taylor received his next orders, the family read them solemnly. He was to take command of Fort Pickering, where his older brother William had been killed by Indians. The fort was located on the border of the Mississippi Territory, near the present site of Memphis, Tennessee.

As Zachary led his wife up the log steps to where the fort sat on a bluff, he could not help but think about William. It was an uncomfortable feeling, even though the Indians of the area were now peaceful and the post was relatively safe. Nonetheless, when their first child was due to be born, Zachary sent Peggy back to Springfield, where she could receive constant care and good treatment. Ann Margaret Mackall Taylor was born on April 9, 1811.

On to Fort Knox

Taylor's next orders were to take charge of Fort Knox, a nest of confusion and discontent. Located on the Wabash River, Fort Knox was the unofficial military headquarters for the Indiana Territory. The fort had been thrown into a state of chaos after its previous commander had killed a subordinate in a duel and then fled the fort.

The soldiers at Fort Knox were understandably upset with the state of affairs that existed there. Moreover, because they were untrained in military offense or defense and undersupplied with weapons and food, they were totally ill-prepared for any possible encounter. Yet they were the back-up unit for General William Henry Harrison, who was leading troops against Indian Chief Tecumseh.

Assisted by the British, Indian tribes had gone on the warpath and were attacking American settlers in the Indiana Territory. Harrison's mission was to vanquish the Indians, drawing upon the forces at Fort Knox for assistance.

With the self-study of military organization fresh in his mind from his extended recuperation, the new commander of Fort Knox was ready to take charge. Carefully, Taylor investigated every possible way the War Department might be of assistance, particularly in providing supplies, and dispatched communications to the appropriate officials in Washington, D.C. He then directed his attention to the discipline and training of his men.

For weeks, Taylor supervised an intense training schedule, insisting upon a minimum level of marksmanship, a mastery of scouting techniques, and a knowledge of marching procedures as well as general self-survival skills. The men grumbled and complained, but beneath their outer discontent grew an appreciation and respect for the man who was teaching them to be true soldiers. Harrison, too, recognized the job Taylor was doing. "In the short time he has been a commander, he has rendered the garrison defensible," the general wrote to the secretary of war in Washington.

More Disappointment

As General Harrison was readying his men for an assault on Tecumseh that he hoped would end the warfare in the Indiana Territory, Taylor was also preparing to lead almost 1,000 men in a supporting attack. Finally, he was going to see action. But it was not to be.

A military court summoned Taylor to New York City to testify at a trial against General Wilkinson, his former commander at New Orleans. The general was charged with dereliction of duty, resulting in a high number of deaths among his troops. He also was under suspicion for consorting with former Vice-President Aaron Burr to establish an independent republic in the Louisiana Territory. Reluctantly, Taylor hurried east to give testimony (Wilkinson was eventually acquitted) and then returned to Fort Knox. By that time, however, the Indians had been defeated, at least for the moment.

Although he had yet to engage actively in a military campaign, Zachary Taylor had achieved some recognition by the War Department. With war between the United States and Great Britain seeming ever more likely, Captain Taylor was assigned to take charge of recruiting in Louisville. Although he had never been fond of the paperwork connected with securing new men for the service, Zachary welcomed the opportunity to spend time at home with his wife and infant daughter. But just four months later, he received orders to reassemble a company of the Seventh Infantry and head to Fort Harrison, an outpost in the Indiana Territory, three miles north of the present city of Terre Haute. Then, on June 18, 1812, the United States declared war on Great Britain.

READY FOR BATTLE

Although the war was officially against England, the actual enemies in many parts of the United States were Indians. Many tribes were angry with the American government for breaking so many of the pacts and treaties it had signed with the Indians years before. Few people had anticipated the rapid expansion of the country westward, and government officials bowed to the wishes of white settlers who wanted land that had been given to the Indians. The tribes stood their ground, however, choosing to fight rather than be pushed out of territories that had been promised to them. They eagerly accepted arms and ammunition from British operating out of Canada.

Fort Harrison, Taylor's new command, was small but strategically located. Only 150 feet square, it sat above a sharp bend in the Wabash River, allowing a perfect view of waterway traffic. Four-feet-deep trenches flanked three sides of the fort, providing ideal shooting positions for those defending the garrison. Blockhouses overlooked both the river and the trenches.

Dispatches reaching Captain Taylor at Fort Harrison were far from cheerful. Combined British and Indian forces were capturing one American fort after another, massacring all defending soldiers. When word reached Taylor that Tecumseh was rallying his forces for an attack against Fort Harrison during the "next full moon," the news was anything but heartening. He had also learned that the Indian chief antici- pated "a large reinforcement."

Taylor took stock of his situation. Many of his men were suffering from fever, and ammunition supplies were low. De- spite these circumstances, Taylor minimized the negatives and emphasized the positives when he sent reports to his superiors. "Morale is high," he noted, "and there is little doubt that we are capable of overcoming any obstacles."

On the morning of September 13, 1812, a small group of Miami Indians brought news that the Tecumseh-led tribes were gathering for an attack on Fort Harrison. That night, four shots rang out in the darkness. Taylor was convinced the sounds spelled the end of two farmers who lived about a quarter of a mile from the fort. His suspicions were confirmed when he sent out a search party the next day and the group returned with the bodies, scalped and mutilated.

That same afternoon, three Shawnee braves approached the fort carrying a white flag. Not wanting them to see the inside of the fort, Taylor met them outside. They claimed to want peace, but the fort commander suspected that they more likely wanted to inspect the inside of the garrison. The In- dians also said there would be no attack that night and that they would return the next day to map out more specific plans for a peaceful settlement. Taylor re-entered the fort, more convinced than ever that the Indians would attack that very evening.

Attack!

Taylor was right. Shortly after 11:00 P.M., he awoke to the sound of gunfire and men yelling. "The blockhouse is afire!" came a shout, and the fort commander raced out into the stockade to see that the building holding the food rations was

indeed blazing. Now that Zachary Taylor was in the midst
of battle he wondered why he had hoped for such an opportunity. But there was no time for idle thoughts: Taylor swung
into action, organizing a bucket brigade to put out the fire.
Then an exploding barrel of whiskey shook the entire garrison, causing two soldiers to flee from the fort. They chose
to risk their lives with the enemy outside rather than face what
they considered certain death inside.

Taylor raced from station to station, quickly analyzing
the situation and shouting orders. Boards were ripped off the
barracks so they would not catch fire. As the women battled
the flames, the men battled the enemy. Outside, the Indians
circled the fort again and again. Now and then one would
try to climb a wall of the stockade, only to be killed by a
musketball. American soldiers fell as well. One soldier stood
up and yelled, "I killed an Indian!" and then slumped to the
ground, cut down by an enemy shot.

The hours slipped by as the fighting continued. The
smoke-filled air was punctuated with the sounds of injured
and dying men. Commander Taylor seemed to be everywhere
at once, directing fire at the enemy, rallying the spirit of men
and women, comforting a fallen soldier, and supervising the
removal of supplies from the burning blockhouse.

A Long Wait

By daybreak, the Indians could see that their plan to burn
down Fort Harrison had failed. But there was more than one
way to achieve victory. The Indians stopped fighting and began a siege. By guarding all land and river roads leading to
the fort, no help could get through. The imprisoned occupants
of the fort could not last long, or so the Indian leaders thought.

What the Indians had not counted on were the strength
and determination of the fort's commander. Taylor established

Taylor's brave and commanding leadership in the defense of Fort Harrison in 1812 made him a national hero and the subject of many heroic tales. (Library of Congress.)

strict rationing of all food, much of which consisted of green corn. Surely, he hoped, word of the attack on Fort Harrison would reach Fort Knox, only 100 miles away. Immediately, troops would be dispatched. It was just a matter of holding on a little bit longer.

But as each day passed, there was no sign of help. Food supplies were getting dangerously low. Finally, Taylor sent two scouts by canoe to try and get help. However, the scouts returned very shortly with bad news. Armed Indian braves were guarding the river, making it impossible for the scouts to get through. If there was no hope by water, perhaps word of their plight could be sent through the woods. Taylor then dispatched two more scouts, but before they had gone very far, 1,200 men arrived under the leadership of Colonel William Russell. It was a weary and relieved Captain Zachary Taylor who welcomed the rescuers.

Russell could hardly believe the stories of how the inhabitants of Fort Harrison had held off the Indian attack, and then survived five additional days of entrapment. Men and women alike pointed to Captain Taylor as the hero of the battle, and Russell conveyed their accounts to General Harrison. Already impressed with Taylor from previous experiences, Harrison was especially pleased to relay news of the unsuccessful Indian attack to President James Madison.

A JOYFUL PRESIDENT; A NEW HERO

Madison, having been bombarded with endless accounts of failed American missions, rejoiced at the news of Taylor's victory. That it was a distant cousin who accounted for the successful undertaking made the news even better. Throughout the country spread the heroic tale of the brave young captain who beat back the Indian attack at Fort Harrison. As a reward for his gallantry in action, on September 12, 1812, Zachary Taylor was brevetted to the rank of major. (A brevet is a temporary promotion in rank given in place of a medal.)

Taylor was pleased with the promotion, but he seemed little aware of the significance of his achievement—had Fort Harrison fallen, a large territory would have been exposed to British and Indian domination. Almost as important was how much Taylor's feat lifted the spirit and hope of American soldiers everywhere. Outnumbered and underequipped, he had made the most of a virtually impossible situation.

The new Major Zachary Taylor had some second thoughts about his success. True, he had long wanted to participate in active military service, to meet and conquer the enemy, to test those tactics of combat that he had heard and read so much about. Yet, now that he had done exactly what he yearned for, he had not anticipated that which now deeply troubled him—the sights and sounds of men dying, his men. Yes, Taylor felt a call to duty, a need to serve his country. But there were some aspects of that service that he knew he would never feel good about.

Chapter 4

Bullets and Battles

His performance at Fort Harrison made Zachary Taylor a national hero at a time when the country needed symbols of courage and daring. He had brought glamour and adventure to the profession of "soldiering." Recruitment figures increased, with many young men wanting to show their own bravery under fire. As for the hero himself, Taylor was assigned as an aide-de-camp to Major General Samuel Hopkins, commander of all the American forces in the Wabash Valley and the Illinois Territory. Taylor welcomed the assignment because the troops included over 2,000 Kentuckians, who looked upon their second-in-command as a brother or cousin.

Despite the friendly feeling, Taylor recognized that the military quality of the men left much to be desired. Most were raw recruits, anxious to become live, unmaimed heroes of battle but lacking any basic military skills. Their inexperience quickly became evident when Hopkins and Taylor led a mission from Fort Knox into the Illinois Territory to remove Indians from the settlements of Peoria and Kickapoo Town along the Illinois River. Scouts got lost as they led the expedition, provisions for the soldiers ran low, and morale plummeted. When volunteers were needed, none stepped forward.

Hopkins decided to return to Fort Knox with his complaining troops rather than taking a chance of running into active combat because he thought most of the men would surely retreat rather than fight. It was a low moment for Taylor, still fresh from witnessing the bravery of his own men at Fort Harrison. The few patrols he personally led found only deserted Indian villages, and when faced with direct enemy encounter, many of his men deserted. He did not challenge Hopkins' decision to return to Fort Harrison in spite of the disappointing expedition. Hopkins, although unhappy with his soldiers and mission, was more than satisfied with his subordinate officer, recording Taylor as "untiring, supportive and respectful."

PEACEFUL INTERLUDE

Obtaining new recruits usually held little interest for the ready-for-action Taylor. But the experience in Illinois made him quite willing to supervise the enlistment of new soldiers in the Indiana and Illinois Territories. He also took charge of drilling procedures but still had time to enjoy the peace and stillness surrounding Fort Knox. Enemy Indian tribes had left the area for northern regions, regrouping with British troops that had suffered numerous defeats and were trying to remobilize in Canada.

During the summer of 1813, Taylor joined Colonel Russell for an Indian-hunting campaign along the Mississinewa River in the Indiana Territory, but the only activity was the burning of a few deserted tribal villages. Taylor was so satisfied with the security of Fort Knox that he encouraged his wife and their young daughter to join him at the outpost. On March 6, 1814, Major and Mrs. Taylor welcomed their second child, another daughter, who they named Sarah Knox Taylor. The choice of the middle name clearly revealed the closeness which Taylor felt for the military, and the new baby was immediately "adopted" as the official mascot of the fort by the soldiers.

ON THE MISSISSIPPI

By late spring, Major Zachary Taylor was eager to test his military prowess beyond the logged walls of Fort Knox. When orders to head west arrived, he was more than ready to go. Huge tribes of Indians were gathering in the Missouri Territory near St. Louis. Recognizing the importance of the Mississippi River, American military leaders feared that the British might be planning to sneak down the river and capture whatever forts they could. At the same time, Indians could be waging land attacks.

Although Taylor was supposed to share command with Brigadier General Benjamin Howard, the latter's sudden illness put all responsibility for the expedition directly in Taylor's hands. Not wasting a moment, he organized a group of 430 militiamen and rangers, loaded them into eight boats, and sailed north up the Mississippi. His ultimate mission was to destroy the Indian villages at the point where the Mississippi and Rock Rivers merged, then to return south and construct a fort at the intersection of the Mississippi and Des Moines Rivers.

It was an ambitious goal, for the hard-fighting Sac and Fox Indians were led by the determined Chief Black Hawk, who had pledged that there would be no white settlements constructed on the upper Mississippi. His own tribal village had been burned at the order of General George Rogers Clark, leading Black Hawk to secure arms and ammunition from the British to wage battle.

Taylor's mission got off to a floundering start. Because the current ran southward, the men frequently had to row the boats. Arms soon wearied from the heavy cargoes of soldiers and supplies. Now and then winds provided some help, but not too often. Within a week, a measles epidemic broke out and many men were unable to work at all. One soldier died. Slowly, however, the boats moved north.

Black Hawk, the crafty Sac and Fox chief, proved an able adversary to the white man along the upper Mississippi River. (Library of Congress.)

Victory and Retreat

By the first week in September 1814, Taylor and his men reached the Rock River. The American commander kept a white flag tied to the bow of the lead boat, hoping that perhaps Indian leaders might come forth and some peaceful agreement might be reached. That did not happen. When one band of warriors rode their horses along the shore and into the shallow water, a naive militiaman suggested that the braves might want to talk. However, the wily Taylor recognized the Indian strategy: pull the Americans close to shore and then ambush the entire brigade.

In addition to the enemy, Taylor also had to deal with the forces of nature. One day, whirling winds and pouring rain suddenly engulfed the boats. Taylor planned to ride out the storm by anchoring the boats in the river, but then he realized that the anchors might not hold and the vessels could be capsized. Seeing an island in the middle of the river, he ordered the men to find safety there. It was a shrewd maneuver, considering both the raging weather and the danger from the enemy on shore. When Taylor ordered as few campfires as possible so as to hide the men's positions, they grumbled at having to eat a cold, damp supper.

Next day, the early morning silence was suddenly broken by the wild shouts and gunfire of attacking Indians. Canoes full of braves were everywhere. As the American soldiers scrambled for cover, Major Taylor ordered the boat that had been armed with swivel guns to set sail. When the swivel guns opened fire, the Indians were driven back to a nearby island, where they took shelter in the underbrush. As the Indians retreated, the swivel guns continued to blast away, picking off one filled canoe after another.

Taylor's victory was short-lived, however. As he and his

men boarded the rest of the boats to continue their journey, a cannonball ripped through the bow of the commander's craft. Along the distant shore, patches of red could be seen. British Redcoats! Not only did the Indians have the Americans outnumbered some four to one, British soldiers were helping them, too. It was not a confrontation Taylor had expected to happen.

Major Taylor quickly analyzed the situation and realized there was no possible hope to beat both the Indians and the British. Indeed, he would be fortunate just to execute an effective retreat. He ordered the boat captains to take their vessels down river. Some three miles south, the Americans pulled their boats ashore and began making repairs.

Taylor was disappointed that he had not been successful in the first stage of his assignment — ridding the Rock River mouthway of Indian encampments. However, he was determined to make good on the second part of his mission — building a fort to protect the St. Louis area. After Taylor selected a site high on the Des Moines River bank, construction began. The men called it Fort Johnson, after Colonel Richard Johnson, who had killed the Indian leader Tecumseh. Spirits ran high among the soldiers as each log was put in place, each nail pounded in.

Before the work could be completed, however, word arrived that Brigadier General Howard was dead — and that Zachary Taylor was needed in St. Louis to assume temporary command of the Missouri Territory. Taylor departed at once, leaving the remaining construction duties in the hands of Captain James Callaway. "We'll dispatch additional men and supplies as soon as possible," Taylor told Callaway. "Continue your work."

In the weeks that followed, Major Zachary Taylor took charge of his new command until Colonel William Russell arrived to relieve him. Taylor then led a troop of men up the Missouri River to strengthen an outpost. When he returned to St. Louis, he was surprised to find Captain Callaway there. He was even more dismayed to learn that Callaway had ordered Fort Johnson to be burned and abandoned because men and supplies had not been sent as promised. To Taylor, Callaway's actions were a clear dereliction of duty because now the British and Indians had a distinct advantage on the Mississippi. But nothing could be done about the situation at this point. However, Taylor vowed that in the future he would never entrust responsibilities to others that he could complete himself.

NO LOOKING BACK

Despite the disappointment over the Fort Johnson mission, Taylor was not one to mull over what was past. Continuing with his duties, he made a few inspection trips on the Mississippi and Missouri Rivers to be sure that settlements along the waterways were adequately protected from possible Indian attack. His awareness of precautionary procedures impressed both military and civilian leaders, and people were quick to take advantage of his suggestions. It was obvious Taylor had learned much through his reading, not only about military combat but the value of readiness in case of an attack.

While doing whatever possible to maintain his soldiers' morale, Taylor himself suffered personal humiliation. He learned that others in military service had been promoted while he had not received a promotion in almost two years. Winfield Scott, who had entered the service at the same time he did and who, in Taylor's view, had not distinguished himself as much, was now a brigadier general. Taylor even conveyed his feelings to his congressman.

PROMOTION AND RESIGNATION

A week after the war of 1812 officially ended on December 24, 1814, with the signing of the Treaty of Ghent, Taylor received word that he had been permanently promoted to major. He was also assigned to the 26th Infantry, which was stationed on the northeastern frontier. Taylor felt that these actions were a reassuring confirmation of the respect in which he was held by the country's military leadership. But he had little opportunity to celebrate the advancement.

After the end of the war, the United States War Department announced that the number of soldiers in the Army would be reduced from 50,000 to 10,000, with a comparable reduction in the number of officers. Of the 216 existing field-grade officers, majors and above like Taylor, only 39 would be retained. Should he wish to accept the position, Taylor was offered one of the 450 captain slots that would remain out of the 2,055 existing at the time.

Furious with the offer, Taylor went to Washington to protest his reduction in rank. He was told by the War Department that through an oversight his promotion to major had not become official until after the war had ended. Thus, with the reduction of Army staff, he was simply not considered a permanent major.

President James Madison even took Taylor's side, noting that Taylor had been the first officer to be brevetted for courage displayed under fire. "The defense of Fort Harrison that led to it, though in an obscure theatre of war, has probably not been exceeded in brilliancy by any affair that has occurred."

Unhappy Exit

Despite Madison's intercession and the War Department's open admission that it had been careless and tardy in authorizing his promotion, the fact remained that the confirmation of Taylor's promotion to the permanent rank of major had not become official until the war was already over. The case was closed.

Taylor could not hide his open disgust at the decision. "One would hope for better treatment from those he has tried to serve with devotion and honor," Zachary wrote to his congressman, Stephen Ormsby. It was a disillusioned Taylor who resigned his commission in the U.S. Army, receiving an honorable discharge and a form letter thanking him for his services.

Chapter 5

Leading Troops Again

To Zachary Taylor, the action of the United States War Department was totally inexcusable and indefensible. It left him angry, confused, and bitter. There was little doubt in his mind when he had first entered the Army that it was to be a career, a lifelong vocation. But the Army had treated him badly, and he felt as if he carried some invisible medal of dishonor.

However, when Taylor returned to his family and friends in Kentucky, he carried the reputation and image of a great war hero. No one was more proud of him than Zachary's own father, Colonel Richard Taylor. The colonel was always telling all who would listen exciting stories about the battles he fought in the Revolutionary War. Now he was the listener as Zachary and three of his other sons described their experiences fighting the British during the War of 1812. Hancock had served as a quartermaster's sergeant in the Army. Joseph, the youngest, also served in the Army as a lieutenant. George had selected the Navy, entering the service as an ensign and departing as a commissioned third lieutenant.

But none of the Taylor sons had distinguished himself like Zachary, who discovered that everyone around Louisville had his own favorite story about "that Taylor" boy who practically won the War of 1812 on his own. It was not merely the Fort Harrison incident about which people spoke with admiration and even awe. Somehow, even the disappointing missions in Illinois and the Missouri Territories had become heroic actions.

In Zachary's mind, however, his Army career had been a failure. But rather than argue with the stories about him that were being circulated, Taylor decided to let people believe whatever they wished. After all, his Army duty was now behind him, and there was the future with Peggy and their two young daughters to think about.

TILLING THE SOIL

For the first time since the land at the mouth of Bluegrass Creek had been given to the Taylors as a wedding gift, Zachary had an opportunity to enjoy it. The methods of farming that he learned from his father returned quickly to Zachary. He eagerly planted a crop of corn and, at his father's suggestion, tried growing tobacco, too, which soon became quite profitable. He also added more comfortable features to the log cabin he had built for his family.

Although there were more than enough slaves to assist with the heavy farm duties at Bluegrass Creek, Zachary was little inclined to sit back and watch others do all the work. "A man can hardly claim to be a farmer if he only provides the land," he wrote to a friend. "I have always welcomed a weary body that comes from a good day's labor."

Despite the long hours in the fields, Taylor cherished the time spent with his wife and two growing girls. Having spent so much time with soldiers, he was not accustomed to the gentle play and warmth shown by Peggy as she cared for their two daughters. It was refreshing, a sight that Zachary enjoyed for hours.

There was time, too, for extended visits with neighbors. For hours Taylor would chat with John Crittenden, agreeing and arguing about the issues of the day. "Those folks in Washington are taking too much power to themselves," Zachary declared. "And consarn it, they're taxing about everything. Seems like while I was in the war, they stuck a tariff on about anything people need." Crittenden nodded his agreement. "But the government needs money, Zach, if it's gonna be strong and carry out programs to help the nation." Taylor shook his head. "Strong, indeed! We fight a war to keep our country strong and once the war is over, the first thing that's done is disassemble the army. That's damn foolishness! If we're going to be strong, we must be ready during peacetime as well as during wartime."

BACK IN UNIFORM

There was little doubt that Taylor still had a substantial interest in military preparedness, despite his honorable discharge from the Army. He was a good farmer—his hearty crops proved that—but his thoughts still frequently drifted back to the time he spent in military service. Soldiering was in his blood, a fact that no one seemed able to recognize more than President Madison. Not content to waste Taylor's military talents, Madison was successful in having his distant cousin recommissioned a major, effective as of May 17, 1816. When news of the appointment reached Taylor, his anger toward and frustration with the U.S. Army disappeared like an early morning fog along a Kentucky hillside. Again Taylor was back in the service. It felt good.

Because Peggy was pregnant again, she could not accompany Taylor to his new post at Fort Howard, which was located at Green Bay, a sidearm of Lake Michigan. Instead of military action, his assignment involved fur-smuggling operations in the area. Using local Winnebago Indians as spies, Taylor broke up the illegal activity and provided protection for the fur traders in the region.

Because Fort Howard was part of the Third Infantry, Taylor reported directly to the commanding colonel at Fort Mackinac. When the colonel took an extended leave, Captain William Pierce became the commanding officer. It made no sense to Taylor that he, a major, should have to seek approval from a captain in order to carry out his duties. He complained about the situation to military officials in Washington, but received no satisfaction.

Internal problems began to plague Fort Howard. Disputes arose about everything from rationing food among the troops to daily assignments for guard duty. A minor argument over whiskey caused Taylor to charge two lieutenants with insubordination, a task he found offensive yet necessary. And the winter weather was bitter; ice blocked Lake Michigan, forcing residents to remain confined at Fort Howard. After 22 months at the post, Taylor was happy to return to Kentucky, where, for the first time, he saw his third daughter, Octavia Pannil Taylor, who had been born on August 16, 1816.

For a year Taylor supervised recruitment in the Louisville area, receiving a promotion to lieutenant colonel during the spring of 1819. The assignment allowed him time to manage the family plantation again and enabled him to be home when a fourth daughter, Margaret Smith Taylor, was born on July 27, 1819. A visit to the Kentucky territory by President James Monroe, who had succeeded Madison in the presidency, was especially exciting because Taylor served as an official host.

Tragedy in Louisiana

In the spring of 1820, however, Zachary Taylor and his family moved south to Louisiana. Soldiers of the Eighth Infantry Regiment were busy at work building a military road that ran 200 miles toward the Gulf of Mexico. Settling his family at Bayou Sara, Taylor began supervising the work crews while also looking over the land for farming possibilities. He and Peggy talked often about making a home for themselves somewhere in the Mississippi Valley, whenever Zach managed to get all the "soldiering out of his system."

Only a few months after their arrival in Bayou Sara, yellow fever swept through the entire area. No home was spared; all the Taylors came down with the disease. A dizzy and weak Zachary Taylor did what he could for his family, but his two youngest daughters could not fight off the infection. Three-year-old Octavia succumbed to the fever on July 8, 1820, while one-year-old Margaret died on October 22. Doctors had little hope of saving their mother, but slowly Peggy Taylor fought her way back from the edge of death. She never fully regained her strength, however, spending the rest of her life as a semi-invalid.

A New Plantation

Once Taylor was strong enough to return to his military duties, he continued supervising the construction of the military road. Then, when the need arose to build Fort Jessup, another fort on the Louisiana frontier, Taylor led a group of men to execute the task. The new fort was completed in 1822.

Continuing his search for a new plantation, Taylor found what he was looking for 45 miles north of Baton Rouge. Not only did the estate boast a handsome mansion and surrounding buildings, it also included 500 acres of prime cotton-growing soil. Shortly after purchasing the property, however, Taylor was sent back to Louisville to bolster recruitment. The national peacetime Army was losing over 10 percent of its enlistees to desertion, largely due to low pay and dissatisfaction with assigned duties.

Before leaving his plantation, Taylor found a suitable man to supervise the 22 slaves working the estate. At the time, Taylor hoped to return soon to Louisiana, but as it turned out, he did not go back there for several years.

Never had Zachary Taylor been in charge of so vast a territory for recruitment, the entire Western Army department. Most of the time he operated out of Cincinnati, leaving Peggy back in Louisville with the rest of the Taylor family. A fifth daughter, Mary Elizabeth, arrived on April 20, 1824, while their last child and only son, Richard, was born on January 27, 1826.

The Political Arena

It was during this time that Taylor became especially interested in politics. His discussions with John Crittenden (on his way to becoming a United States senator and governor of Kentucky) about political issues were still lively and spirited. Taylor noted that in the struggle for power there were often similarities between the War Department and the presidency. "Manipulation" seemed to play a key role – how one man or his supporters handled internal maneuvering.

It was while impatiently waiting for his own promotion from lieutenant colonel to colonel, that Taylor watched with some distaste how the presidential race of 1824 was decided. It was a contest among four individuals, each representing a different faction of the Democratic-Republican Party. Andrew Jackson of Tennessee polled the most votes in the general election and collected 99 electoral votes. John Quincy Adams garnered 84 electoral votes, William Harris Crawford obtained 41, while Henry Clay captured 37. Because no candidate won a clear majority of electoral votes, the choice was to be made by the members of the House of Representatives from among the three leading contenders. Clay's supporters in the House cast their votes for Adams, thus securing a spot for Clay as Adams' secretary of state. "It's not the best way," Taylor told his friend Crittenden. "It's the only way we've got for now," replied Crittenden.

Although politics intrigued Zachary Taylor, he had little time or opportunity to play an active political role. Because he moved so often from one place to another on military assignments, he failed to establish residency so that he might even vote in an election. After being assigned to a number of different garrisons, the year 1829 found Taylor in command of Fort Snelling, an outpost near the present city of St. Paul, Minnesota. The following year, he was assigned to Fort Crawford at Prairie du Chien in the Wisconsin wilderness, where he supervised the building of a new structure to replace the old one. Like other military installations of the time, both Fort Snelling and Fort Crawford were being improved so they would be better able to withstand possible attack by hostile Indians.

Catching a Punch

After "far too long a wait," Zachary Taylor was made a full colonel in 1832. Seldom did he allow for any celebrating, but in this case, he joined his men in a festive party. But the next day, when it was back to business as usual, a most unusual incident occurred.

During a dress parade, in which uniformed soldiers display drilling techniques and weapons-handling skills, Taylor noticed that one new recruit was particularly clumsy. The soldier, unknown to Taylor, was a German who barely understood the English language. When the recruit stood improperly in line while being inspected, Taylor approached him directly, took hold of the man's ears, and began shaking him. Others had suffered similar punishment at Taylor's hands, a physical reprimand called "wooling."

The recruit would not accept such treatment. After breaking loose of Taylor's hands, he landed a fist on the commander's jaw. A stunned Taylor instantly found himself in the dirt, while nearby officers and soldiers fixed their guns on the recruit. This was mutiny, after all, punishable by death. But Taylor, scrambling to his feet, would have none of it. "Let the man alone!" he ordered, still rubbing his chin. "He will make a good soldier." It was such understanding and respect for his men that won Zachary Taylor their everlasting admiration.

FACING AN OLD ENEMY

In May of 1832, Colonel Zachary Taylor was summoned to engage an old enemy of the past. Once more, Chief Black Hawk of the Sac and Fox Indians threatened to limit westward expansion of American settlers. In truth, the white man had encroached upon lands long held by the Indians in the northwest Illinois Territory. After being driven across the Mississippi River into Iowa, the tribes decided to return to their previously held homeland. When white homesteaders challenged their re-entry, there was bloodshed.

A call went out for help. General Henry Atkinson and Colonel Zachary Taylor were given the assignment to assemble a group of Illinois militia and regular soldiers. (The Illinois volunteers included a man named Abraham Lincoln.) Recalling his unsuccessful encounter with the wily Black Hawk some 20 years before, Taylor vowed that this time the outcome would be different. His orders were to "pursue Black Hawk until he is captured." The determined colonel would settle for no less.

It was no easy task. Although greatly outnumbered by

the American troops, the Sac chief proved to be an excellent military tactician. He possessed an uncanny ability to patiently outwait his adversaries, build up their tensions and fear, then strike swiftly. Often the attacks would come from the rear, while the soldiers were poised for a frontal attack. Black Hawk knew the territory well, and his warriors were willing to fight to the death for him.

Taylor, on the other hand, faced numerous problems. Because the territory was relatively unknown to him and his soldiers, they often found themselves threatened by ambush. Moreover, area militiamen, most of whom had little preparation for warfare, had enlisted for only 30 days of service. After that, they were no longer obligated to remain on active duty. As a result, by the time they had been suitably drilled and trained, many of the area militiamen chose to return to their homes.

Not only were the Illinois militiamen entitled to leave their military duties at the end of their 30-day enlistment periods, they were also under no obligation to journey beyond state limits. When Black Hawk and the nucleus of his warriors started to head north in canoes, the Illinois militiamen balked at following. But after Taylor applied pressure through verbal threats, the soldiers, one and all, got into flatboats and went after the Indians.

But the waterways only went so far. As the Indians headed into Wisconsin, the chase continued on foot and horseback in blistering heat. Unused to such travel, the soldiers begged to stop. Taylor refused, the orders to capture Black Hawk pounding in his mind. Through treacherous marshes, "over hills that in Europe would be termed 'mountains,' " Taylor wrote, he pushed onward. There was no pausing for those men unable to continue because of illness or exhaustion. They were merely left to fend for themselves until they recovered, after which they were ordered to rejoin the expedition.

The Enemy Fights Back

The Indians, too, suffered from the prolonged journey. Weak from travel and lack of supplies, they relied on the spirit and determination that Black Hawk seemed to provide without end. At a place called Wisconsin Heights, the Indians encountered troops under the command of General James Henry. Not only did the braves display their usual heroic fighting spirit, but the squaws and children moved supplies and equipment while bullets sailed past them. As Indian warriors returned the white man's fire, their wives and children crossed the Rock River in hastily built small boats.

Jefferson Davis, an American lieutenant who would later become Taylor's son-in-law as well as president of the Confederacy during the Civil War, wrote with glowing admiration of the Indians' courage and resourcefulness. "Had it been performed by white men," wrote Davis, "it would have been immortalized as one of the most splendid achievements in military history." Outnumbered two to one and caught completely without warning, the Indians had managed a daring retreat at the cost of only 68 braves.

But retreat it was, however heroic. And it was clear that the fleeing Indians could not continue much farther. Tired and hungry, they traveled along the Mississippi River, the friendly waters that they knew and loved so well. Meanwhile, American soldiers charted their own plans, being careful not to underestimate the shrewd planning and brave fighting of their adversary.

A Battle Ends

By early August 1832, the end was near. In command of the Sixth Infantry Regiment, Zachary Taylor joined with other forces to surround Black Hawk's band along the Mississippi in the rugged Wisconsin woodland. From Prairie du Chien, the Army vessel *Warrior,* loaded with guns, made its way up the Mississippi, ready to join in the attack against the Indians.

In a final desperate ploy, Black Hawk and several of his warriors positioned themselves high above the riverbanks in full view of the American soldiers. It appeared that he was overseeing the evacuation of the main body of his people up-river, when, in truth, the Indians were attempting to retreat downstream. The plan worked until a small scouting party of American soldiers discovered the trick. In the battle that followed, known as the Battle of Bad Axe, the Indians had little chance for victory, especially when guns from the *Warrior* sent barrages of shells into their midst.

Taylor, leaping from his horse, waded to an island where he could command an unrestricted view of the action and direct his men accordingly. One by one the Indians were killed or captured. Black Hawk himself was captured soon afterwards and eventually taken to Washington, where he promised President Andrew Jackson that he would live in peace for the rest of his life. Black Hawk kept his promise.

With the defeat of Black Hawk's forces, Zachary Taylor returned to Fort Crawford, happy to join his family for a rest. However, he made no effort to hide his disgust with the overall handling of the Black Hawk War. "The entire affair was bungled," he wrote, although he hesitated to place blame directly for a war that cost some 1,000 lives and $3 million.

The waste of human life troubled Taylor deeply, largely because he felt those administrators far away in Washington had never witnessed the tragedy of sudden and terrifying death. At 47, Zachary Taylor was fully convinced that his country, like any country that expected to remain free and independent, needed to maintain an active and trained army. But after the amount of bloodshed he had personally witnessed, Taylor was just as convinced that any sensible nation should avoid war, if at all possible.

Chapter 6

Indians on the Warpath

During the next five years, troubles in the northwest frontier were minimal. This enabled Zachary Taylor, the commander of Fort Crawford, to peacefully supervise the territory while building new roads in the area as western expansion continued.

The quiet times also allowed recruits to be trained in a manner that Taylor approved, and he kept a careful eye on the entire procedure. "I've seen too many men sent into battle before they learned to shoot," he told those in charge of the newcomers. "A poorly trained soldier is worth more to an enemy than he is to us. Anyone entering this fort as a recruit while I am in command shall leave here equipped to carry out any military mission. I hope I make myself clear."

SOLDIERS COMPARED

Taylor was clearly understood, as well as being firm and fair. And yet, within a sturdy and stout exterior, Zachary Taylor had mellowed a bit. Visits from General Winfield Scott, nick-

"Old Fuss and Feathers" General Winfield Scott was a contrast in soldiering style to the more informal Zachary Taylor. (Library of Congress.)

named "Old Fuss and Feathers," provided an intriguing comparison of style. Both Taylor and Scott had entered service at the same time in 1808, and both had seen considerable action. But whereas Taylor had learned his soldiering as he went, Scott could boast—and often did—of his West Point background and education. He put much importance on appearances, feeling that the uniform an individual wore reflected his entire being. Scott felt that anything less than clean and spotless was an insult to the country a soldier represented.

Scott also believed that every detail of battle had to be checked and doublechecked before actively engaging the enemy. Although Taylor agreed with that theory, circumstances did not always provide time for detailed analysis before acting. Taylor placed heavy emphasis on immediate action and reaction, recognizing that there was often much to be gained from not waiting too long. "Locate the objective, attack, and win!" was his motto.

As to an officer's or soldier's appearance, Taylor insisted on regulations being maintained. But far more important was what was *inside* the man—the ability to think and act with courage—than how immaculately he presented himself.

LIFE AT FORT CRAWFORD

Fort Crawford provided Zachary Taylor, his wife and family, and others within the outpost an opportunity to enjoy life. Visitors to the fort found themselves invited to dine with the commander, who was more than willing to share the fine wines provided officers of his rank. Not that Taylor encouraged drinking. Far from it. Any soldier found intoxicated at the post, whether on or off duty, met with a stern lecture from the fort's commander.

Taylor encouraged the development of a fort library, frequently using the facility himself. Books were sparse, but eagerly read and openly shared. One of the barracks buildings was converted to a theater, and Taylor enjoyed escorting his family to amateur productions presented by those at the post. Dances were held, too, with Taylor clapping to the fiddler's playing and laughing with pleasure.

Family Problems

The laughter faded, however, when Taylor became aware that his daughter Sarah was showing a romantic interest in Lieutenant Jefferson Davis. In 1829, while at Fort Snelling, Taylor's oldest daughter, Ann, fell in love and married the post surgeon, Dr. Robert Cooke Wood. As a professional soldier, Taylor disapproved of such marriages. He felt that the sacrifices and disappointments of a soldier's wife far outnumbered her rewards. His own wife, Peggy, could do nothing to alter his convictions.

At least Dr. Wood had graduated from medical school and had the maturity of being 12 years older than Ann. Davis, on the other hand, possessed a West Point background (hardly a plus factor in Taylor's mind), was only six years older than Sarah, and was known to be somewhat reckless. At one wedding ceremony at the fort, Davis had chosen to dance with an Indian girl. This angered the girl's brother, who drew a knife, causing Davis to pull a gun in self-defense. Taylor interceded, calming the situation, but he did not forgive Davis' behavior.

After Taylor became aware that Davis was interested in his daughter, he was outraged. "I'll be damned if another daughter of mine shall marry into the army!" Taylor shouted. "I know enough of the family life of soldiers. I scarcely know my own children, or they me."

Sarah Taylor and Jefferson Davis chose to ignore her father's feelings, however. On the pretext of returning to Kentucky for a family visit, Sarah married Lieutenant Davis on June 17, 1835. It was a saddened Taylor who received the news, but he was momentarily pleased when he learned that his new son-in-law had resigned his Army commission.

After the newlyweds went to live at the Davis plantation near Vicksburg, Mississippi, a deadly fever struck the area. To escape the sickness, they then traveled to Louisiana to stay with relatives there. Unfortunately, it was too late, for both of them became ill with the fever. Less than three months after her marriage, Sarah Knox Taylor Davis died. The news left her father numbed with grief.

SEMINOLE UPRISING

Taylor remained at Fort Crawford until 1837, when he was again needed to put down another Indian uprising. This time it was the Seminoles in Florida, which the United States had acquired from Spain in 1819. The Indians were actively resisting the encroachment of their lands by white settlers. The tribes also harbored runaway slaves from southern plantations. The Seminoles were known to be willing to die for what they believed, spurred on by their young leader, Osceola.

An earlier attempt to drive the Indians from their Florida homelands had met with violence and death. "You have guns," Osceola wrote to Brigadier General Duncan Clinch, who had been sent to settle the dispute, "and so have we. You have powder and lead, and so have we. You have men, and so have we. Your men will fight, and so will ours, till the last drop of Seminole's blood has moistened the dust of his hunting ground."

Although Osceola was captured, his braves continued to wage war. Clearly, Zachary Taylor knew that his mission to Florida would not be an easy one. He had orders to take charge of every military outpost southeast of Tampa Bay and conduct whatever military operations were necessary to subdue the Indians.

Never did Taylor prepare more carefully for a military encounter than in Florida. During the daylight hours, he met the soldiers arriving in Tampa Bay, checked and doublechecked supplies, and made certain that the wagons were in good repair and that the donkeys were well fed and strong. At night, he reviewed every map he could get, becoming as familiar as possible with the grasslands and swamps of the territory.

Recognizing the amount of time that might be wasted waiting for supply trains to catch up to his troops, Taylor charted an innovative plan of action. Where there were already established forts, he ordered provisions sent ahead to them. Where strategically located forts could be quickly built, he had crude but usable outposts constructed.

Before proceeding with his plan, however, Taylor made a final effort to settle matters peacefully. In the absence of the captured chief Osceola, leadership of the Indians had fallen to two of his assistants, Oulatooshee and Jumper. Taylor met with the two Seminoles, encouraging them to take their people westward and avoid further bloodshed. "Osceola has spoken for us," the leaders answered, refusing all offers of a peaceful compromise.

A Rugged Journey

Taylor then put his plan into operation, sending supplies ahead to established forts and building forts where needed. However, although he had carefully studied the terrain, Taylor had underestimated the constant dangers posed by snakes and alligators. And the mosquitoes were so thick that they created a blinding screen in some parts of the murky swamps. The dense forest of cypress trees created an additional hardship.

With each mile his troops moved inland, Taylor knew they were in territory far more familiar to the Seminoles than to him. Nonetheless, he gave the command to keep moving. Wherever needed, in case of retreat, bridges and depots for storing supplies were hastily constructed.

Small clusters of Seminoles were captured, but Taylor had no intention of returning to permanent safety until the main body of Indians was found. That occurred on December 25, 1837. Led by Indian guides, Taylor came upon a group of some 700 warriors camped on the north shore of Lake Okeechobee. Nestled on a cypress-covered hillside, the Indians enjoyed the advantage of nature's camouflage for hiding. And their position was unreachable except by walking through a foot-deep mud swamp, wide open for shooting.

Although he was aware of the potential danger of a headlong frontal attack, Taylor also realized there was no other way of engaging the enemy. But if his men were going to face death, so would he. Taylor joined his troops as they sloshed through the mud toward the waiting Seminoles. His men drew courage from their commander's bravery.

To the enemy, Taylor could not be identified as an officer to be shot at. He wore a straw hat and coveralls, looking more like a farmer than a colonel in the United States Army. It was just one more factor that endeared Taylor to his troops — there was nothing fancy about his style. He slept around campfires with his men, ate the same rations they did, and fought side-by-side with them.

Death at Lake Okeechobee

As shots rang out across the swampland, American soldiers sank into the mud. Here and there a frightened man would break from the line approaching the Indians and run away. But most remained, many crouching and returning the gunfire. Taylor shouted commands, mostly to make his presence and spirit felt.

As the hours passed, American casualties continued to mount. Taylor ordered a footbridge be built so that the dead and wounded could be carried away from the front lines. Seeing so many of his men killed or injured, the saddened commander pushed his troops even harder so that a victory might be achieved as soon as possible.

Finally, with one last round of gunfire, the Seminoles took flight. They could see that any further fighting was useless – the American soldiers had no intention of giving up. The Battle of Lake Okeechobee was a victory for Zachary Taylor, but "dearly purchased." The bodies of only a dozen Indians were found (a somewhat misleading number because the Seminoles took their dead with them), while the Americans lost 28 and counted 122 wounded. The success of Taylor and his troops at Lake Okeechobee became even more apparent somewhat later, when the Seminoles finally decided to surrender rather than continue the fighting.

A FOOL OR A HERO?

In 1838 Zachary Taylor was promoted to Brevet Brigadier General by the United States War Department. However, not everyone praised his actions at the Battle of Lake Okeechobee. Some claimed he had placed a string of Missouri Volunteers on the front line of attack, thereby protecting his regular trained soldiers. Senator Thomas Hart Benton of Missouri went so far as to label Taylor "a fool," but only those from Missouri seemed to agree. Thomas S. Jessup, a respected general in the War Department, labeled the Battle of Okeechobee "one of the best-fought battles in American military history." And President Martin Van Buren publicly commended Taylor for his actions, inviting him to Washington, D.C., where he personally could thank Taylor on behalf of the nation.

Interestingly, Zachary Taylor felt the policy of forcing the Seminoles to move west was totally unjust. But he was a soldier, trained to take orders. He helped supervise the movement of thousands of Seminole Indians to reservations west of the Mississippi Rivers. However, despite all efforts to destroy any remaining Seminole influence by burning their small villages, pockets of resistance continued in the Florida peninsula.

Although Taylor was officially replaced as a military commander in Florida in April of 1839, he remained a year longer, acting as an Indian agent. Upon completion of his duties, Taylor received glowing praise from Secretary of War Joel Poinsett. He said that the Florida campaign had been carried out "with vigor and ability under that zealous and indefatigable officer Brig. General Taylor, who accomplished all that could be expected with the very limited means at his command."

A New Nickname

Taylor looked upon his military efforts in Florida with complete satisfaction. He felt that the Missouri criticism was completely unjust while the glowing words of tribute were a bit exaggerated. On his own account, Taylor felt there had been a job to do, he had done it as well as he could, and now it was over.

Perhaps what Taylor appreciated most was the praise from his own men, those with whom he had shared day-to-day struggles. They nicknamed him "Old Rough and Ready"—an affectionate label reflecting the honor and respect with which his soldiers held him.

Chapter 7
From East to West

The Florida campaign had taken its toll on Taylor. Always able to avoid injury from enemy gunfire, he enjoyed no such luck with a constant sickness, probably malaria. Since his early days as a soldier, when he first caught the disease, it frequently made him weak and shaky. During his two years fighting the Seminoles, he was often ill, but he would not give in to the sickness for fear of weakening the spirit and morale of his men.

The military leaders in Washington noticed Taylor's gaunt and pasty look when he arrived there to file his final reports on the Florida campaign. Concerned about his health, they encouraged Taylor to seek immediate rest and recuperation. It was advice the tired soldier was glad to take.

For the next six months Taylor enjoyed traveling leisurely with Peggy by his side. They returned to Louisville to visit relatives there. Then daughter Betty took time off from boarding school in Philadelphia to join her parents for a trip to New York City and Niagara Falls. It was good to be away from the sounds of rifles, the smell of gunpowder, and the sight of death. Slowly, Zachary Taylor regained his health. He also managed to push some of his more depressing memories to the back of his mind.

A "DREAM HOME"

Having no desire to return to Florida after his leave was over, Taylor requested an assignment near Baton Rouge. He knew Peggy liked the area, and he hoped to look for additional land investments. His request was granted. Weary of the quarters provided by the Army to an officer and his family, Peggy Taylor chose instead a rather rundown cottage overlooking the Mississippi River. She promised her husband that she would convert it into their "dream home."

While his wife pursued a relatively active home life (the illness which claimed two of their children never allowed Peggy Taylor to enjoy very good health), Taylor's task of supervising Army troops in the area was slow-paced and uneventful. After the election of William Henry Harrison in 1840, Taylor was flattered when the newly chosen President sought his advice about Cabinet appointments. Both men were generals, both believed in a strong federal government over the rights of individual states, and both generally accepted the policies advocated by the Whig Party.

Of all the choices for Harrison's Cabinet, Taylor was strongest in his support of John Bell of Tennessee for the office of secretary of war. Bell seemed willing to recognize the importance of a well-trained Army in war *and* peacetime, a top priority to Taylor. Taylor was gratified when his recommendation was accepted. However, Harrison's death only a few weeks after his inauguration was a stunning blow to his fellow soldier in Baton Rouge.

Thoughts of Retirement

At 57, Zachary Taylor began to give more and more thought to his retirement from the Army. His frame of mind caused him to look for possible financial investments that would provide security and comfort to Peggy and himself in their old age. Late in 1841, he purchased some 2,000 acres at Cypress Grove, just north of Baton Rouge. The land was prime cotton soil, despite its tendency to flood, and the plantation was well run by slaves.

Knowing his Army duties would not allow him to give the plantation the attention it required, Taylor hired a fair and firm overseer to manage the property. "Treat the workers well," the new owner instructed. "See that they are well fed, well clothed and well cared for. If they be sick, let them rest until they are well again." It was the same kindness that he had watched his father display years ago at Springfield. Taylor even gave a bonus of a few dollars to each slave at Christmas time.

Taylor's peaceful interlude came to an end when he was asked to take command of the Second Military Department, the headquarters for which were located at Fort Gibson, deep in Indian territory. However, the commandant he was replacing suggested that Taylor and his wife might be more comfortable at Fort Smith, in the Arkansas Territory. Upon visiting Fort Gibson, Taylor agreed.

PADDING THE EXPENSES

It was not long after Taylor took command of the Second Military Department that he realized he had another major enemy on his hands—waste. Having fought in military campaigns where shortages of supplies, ammunition, and weapons were common, Taylor was shocked to find money being spent recklessly and without purpose. "It is apparent that the farther one is from Washington, the more inclined he is to want to pick the nation's coffers," he wrote to a friend.

Expenses were being padded on road and bridge construction. When a fort wall was built, it was built twice the size needed. Some forts were being maintained due more to the pressure and pleasure of influential traders and saloon keepers than to any practical need. Yet there were places where forts were needed but none existed.

After Taylor carefully inspected the entire area of Louisiana, Arkansas, and Oklahoma over which he had jurisdiction, he then proposed changes. Officials in Washington heeded his advice, knowing the long-time military leader would not be making suggestions without good cause.

His location offered Taylor many opportunities to deal personally with Indian chiefs and tribes. Even those who had fought "the great white general" in the past respected him. "He stays with his men and fights," observed one Seminole who had been relocated with his people after the Florida uprising. "Most white generals sit on horses far away and watch, or maybe hide in bushes. Not this white general. He brave." Recognizing his personal appeal and influence, Taylor met often with various Indian chiefs. He tried to maintain peaceful relations between tribes as well as with the American soldiers and pioneers moving west.

"AN ARMY OF OBSERVATION"

Of major concern and demanding the most delicate attention was the Texas area. Once under Mexican control, the Texans had gained their independence in 1836, and officially, Texas was a republic. However, most of its people, including its president, Sam Houston, favored annexation to the United States. So did President John Tyler of the United States, who had succeeded William Henry Harrison in office.

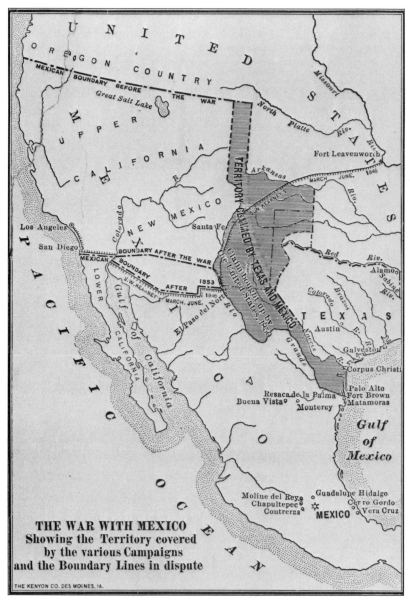

THE WAR WITH MEXICO
Showing the Territory covered
by the various Campaigns
and the Boundary Lines in dispute

THE KENYON CO. DES MOINES, IA.

*Taylor was assigned to command an "army of observation" as
the border dispute between the United States and Mexico
caused relationships between the two countries to become more
and more strained. (Library of Congress.)*

As negotiations between Texan and U.S. officials began in 1843, Taylor was ordered to command "an army of observation" so that Mexico would not be inclined to attempt any kind of forceful action. The negotiating process was not expected to move swiftly, and Mexico had pledged to attack Texas if it annexed itself to the United States.

No final action had been taken on the annexation issue before campaigning began for the 1844 presidential election. Opponents of slavery opposed Texas' admission to the Union because many landowners in the republic held slaves. If left to the negotiators, a treaty might have been agreed to early in the year. But once the matter of slavery started receiving major attention, it was certain to become a political issue. Taylor and his troops kept a careful watch, not wanting to create any problem that might jeopardize the ongoing negotiating process.

Summertime found the commander of "the army of observation" suffering once again from "bilious fever." The short-legged general never had found it easy to mount a horse. Now, in his weakened condition, he had to be lifted aboard. He ignored Peggy's warning to conserve his strength, nor would he listen to his aides, who suggested a long period of complete bedrest.

Taylor was not about to start pampering himself now, after so many years of pushing himself to fulfill his duties whenever he became sick. To his soldiers, the general looked like a battered scarecrow with his sunken cheeks and death-like pallor, outfitted in his usual garb of baggy cotton pants, straw hat, and long linen coat. "It sure ain't Fuss and Feathers Scott!" some would laugh, drawing a weak smile from their leader. "You should be glad it isn't!" Taylor drawled back.

TENSION IN THE AIR

James Knox Polk won the presidential election of 1844, running on a political platform calling for the annexation of Texas. It was clear that U.S. leaders supported entry of the new state, and there was every indication that Texas leaders wanted the same thing. Mexican officials, however, remained adamant in their threats to attack should annexation win approval.

Zachary Taylor could not relax his guard, although he grew weary of the waiting process. He longed to return to Louisiana, to see for himself how his plantation at Cypress Grove was being managed. And both father and mother hoped to personally be on hand to watch Richard, their only son, graduate from Yale University. Throughout his Army career, Taylor suffered from feelings of guilt because his military duties kept him from sharing the pleasures of family life. Richard, in particular, scarcely had an opportunity to get to know his seldom-present father. Now, Zachary wanted desperately to establish a true relationship with his son.

In March of 1845, the U.S. Congress passed a joint resolution approving the annexation of Texas to the Union. Now, all that remained was for Texans to show their support for annexation. Again, however, the Mexican government sent ominous warnings northward – annexation meant trouble.

Secretary of State James Buchanan would not be intimidated. He sent word that should the people of Texas choose to join the Union, the United States would provide appropriate defense against any foreign power. There was no misunderstanding the directive. If Zachary Taylor entertained any serious notions about leaving his position for any private family business, such thoughts were quickly put aside. He knew where he was needed – no one had to tell "Old Rough and Ready" that.

Getting into Position

During the summer of 1845, American troops assembled along the Texas-Mexico border, ready for any action. Analyzing the military situation, Taylor took his troops to the mouth of the Nueces River at Corpus Christi, a strategic location in case of a Mexican attack.

By September, almost 4,000 soldiers were quartered at Corpus Christi, half of the entire United States Army. The territory became a city of tents. Living conditions quickly deteriorated with the passing of autumn into winter. Gone were the idle days when the men could enjoy deer hunting and bathing in the Gulf of Mexico.

Winter storms soon soaked the mile-long tent city, and icy winds caused the strongest of men to shake and shiver. Sanitation problems developed, leading to outbreaks of diarrhea and dysentery. The miserable conditions led to short tempers, causing fights to break out among the men. "Soldiers need to be active and busy," Taylor wrote in a journal. "Waiting is never wise if it continues for too long."

In one sense, the village of Corpus Christi prospered, catering to the thousands of soldiers camped nearby. Whiskey flowed freely in saloons, dance halls featured loud music and loose women. Professional gamblers enjoyed taking money from naive soldiers. Rules for the servicemen were strict and numerous, but some officers refused to enforce them. Because he went to bed early every evening, Taylor was unaware of much of the nighttime activity. If he learned of any military disobedience, resignations were demanded immediately.

On December 29, 1845, Texas voted for annexation, making it the 28th state of the Union. All land north of the Rio Grande River was considered part of the United States. Secretary of War William L. Marcy directed Taylor to take his troops to the Rio Grande, but there was to be no action beyond that. "It is not designed in our present relations with Mexico, that you should treat her as an enemy," Marcy emphasized, "But, should she resume that character, by a declaration of war, or any open act of hostility toward us, you will not act merely on the defensive, if your relative means enable you to do otherwise." It was typical Washington bureaucratic language. Simply stated, it meant, "Do not attack, but if attacked, be ready to fight back!"

Chapter 8

War with Mexico

Not all the preparations and planning for war with Mexico revolved around land operations. While Taylor and others carefully analyzed the possibilities of attack and engagement in Texas itself, attention was also given to the use of U.S. naval vessels. During the negotiations between the United States and Mexico, American ships had been withdrawn from Mexican waters. It was hoped that President José Joaquin de Herrera might back away from earlier threats and that matters could be peacefully resolved. But Herrera's overthrow by General Mariano Parades squelched any such hope.

Parades was a warrior, little interested in or knowledgeable about diplomacy. Recognizing this, official orders went out from Washington to Taylor and others commanding land troops. Naval vessels were also sent back to Mexican coastal waters in case war broke out. Strategic ports on the Gulf of Mexico, such as Tampico and Veracruz, were vital to the Americans, as were Mexican port cities on the Pacific coast.

Receiving his orders to proceed to the Rio Grande, Taylor felt no need for haste. It was still early February, and the 180-mile journey from Corpus Christi would be difficult in the winter. Scouting parties brought back reports of bad roads. Moreover, Taylor's orders distinctly stated to proceed "as soon as it can be conveniently done with reference to the season and the routes by which your movements must be made."

In truth, too, this was not a military campaign about which Zachary Taylor had strong convictions. In fact, he had spoken publicly and strongly against the annexation of Texas, a position shared by the majority of Whigs in Washington. He had only gradually warmed to the idea over a period of time.

Nonetheless, Taylor was a soldier, honor-bound to do his duty. That included exercising caution to ensure his men's safety. But there were many who had grown impatient with the long confinement at Corpus Christi. When the news began to circulate among the troops that orders had finally arrived to move, there were those who wanted to do so immediately. Taylor stood firm, however. "I shall give the command," he declared, and there was no one who would challenge the outspoken, crusty general to his face.

MARCHING TO THE RIO GRANDE

On Sunday, March 8, 1846, the American soldiers broke camp and began the trek to the Rio Grande. The first few days of the march were uneventful. Taylor was greatly pleased with the discipline of the men and the time they were making after being idle for so long. Then a 65-mile stretch of sandy desert under a blazing sun tested the endurance of even the strongest man in uniform. Water was carefully rationed, never being enough to soothe parched throats and blistered lips.

Reaching the Arroyo Colorado, a shallow salt water lagoon, the American soldiers stopped. Across the 100-yard wide lagoon stood Mexican soldiers, armed and on patrol. When notified of their presence, Taylor seemed unconcerned. He ordered his men to cut away part of the bluff leading down to the lagoon so that the 300 wagons could have clear passage. As for the Mexicans, he sent a scout under a white flag to tell them that he planned to cross the lagoon the next morning and that he expected no interference. By the next morning, the Mexican soldiers were gone, and the American troops continued on their journey.

It took almost three weeks for Taylor's troops to reach the Rio Grande. Their arrival hardly went unnoticed. Across the river, in the town of Matamoros, Mexican lookouts watched every move of the American troops while they hastily constructed a stockade. During the next two weeks, activity on both sides of the river seemed to be in unison as the two sides prepared for battle. The Mexicans mounted guns aimed at the American stockade, while four 18-pound American guns were zeroed in on the Matamoros town square, the center of the Mexican unit. Then came the waiting, waiting for one side or the other to make a mistake—a mistake that would explode both forces into open battle.

THE WAR BEGINS

When Taylor received word that the chief quartermaster of the American forces had been found slain, immediate suspicion was cast on the Mexicans. Yet there was no proof, and no body discovered. When a search party was sent out to investigate, the group was ambushed and two Americans were killed.

Before any retaliatory action could be taken, Taylor received an ultimatum from Mexican General Pedro de Ampudia demanding that the American troops retreat to the north bank of the Nueces River within 24 hours. An angry Taylor sent back a curt message: "The instructions under which I am acting will not permit me to retrograde from the position I now occupy." But before he could do anything about Taylor's refusal to retreat, de Ampudia was removed from his command. Tension continued on both sides of the Rio Grande.

Late in April Taylor received word that a large force of Mexican cavalry had crossed the Rio Grande some 30 miles from the American camp. He immediately dispatched a scouting party of 63 dragoons under the leadership of Captain Seth Thornton. It was essential to know exactly how many Mexicans were involved and what they were planning to do. Misled by a treacherous scout, Thornton soon found his group surrounded by some 1,600 Mexican soldiers led by General Anastasio Torrejon. Not content to merely take prisoners, the Mexicans attacked, either shooting the Americans or clubbing them to death as they tried to escape. A few prisoners were taken for bargaining possibilities.

Learning of the attack, Taylor sent off an immediate communication to President James Knox Polk. "Hostilities may now be considered as commenced," the American general curtly noted.

The Battle of Palo Alto

Informed that the Mexicans, led by General Mariano Arista, planned to attack the American supply center in nearby Port Isabel, Taylor took the initiative and marched his troops there. Shortly after leaving their position across from Matamoros, the Americans heard the sounds of cannons in the distance as the Mexicans attacked their former outpost.

A determined Taylor sent word to Washington: "If the enemy oppose my march, in whatever force, I shall fight him." His courageous words and actions brought civilians swarming into recruitment centers to enlist in the Army. They were welcome additions, as Taylor needed reinforcements.

Nearing a water hole at Palo Alto on the way to Port Isabel, Taylor found himself facing a Mexican blockade. It was hardly an even match – 2,200 American soldiers against some 6,100 Mexicans! If ever Taylor had to exhibit superior leadership, it was here at Palo Alto. Quickly he positioned his infantry and artillery. American soldiers raced from spot

It was a strong belief of Zachary Taylor that, during battle, military leaders should appear collected and calm so as to instill confidence in their troops. An artillery lieutenant sketched this picture of "Old Rough and Ready" during the Battle of Palo Alto. (Library of Congress.)

to spot, loading their rifles, gathering their courage. There would be no turning back.

In the midst of all the activity was "Old Rough and Ready" Zachary Taylor sitting on his horse Old Whitey. Calmly chewing tobacco, he would pause now and then to give an order. "How can he look so calm?" one infantryman asked another. No one had an answer, yet there is little doubt that Taylor's apparent confidence and relaxed manner contributed greatly to raising the morale of his soldiers.

Finally, Taylor's troops moved forward at their commander's direction. Mexican artillerymen immediately opened fire. As American cannons responded, it was clear to see the difference in accuracy. Taylor's insistence on quality marksmanship quickly paid rich dividends. Mexican soldiers toppled everywhere, cut down by the deadly accuracy of the American artillery. Mexican cannonballs, however, hissed harmlessly overhead, seldom striking their targets. "We're blastin' them, boys!" one American artilleryman shouted as the American soldiers cheered in frenzied delight.

Suddenly attention focused on a row of Mexican cavalry charging the Americans' right flank. Again Taylor shouted orders, commanding the riflemen and cannon crews to direct their fire at the Mexicans racing forward on their horses. Again with deadly accuracy, the Americans blasted away at the approaching horsemen. Down they went, with each fallen cavalryman drawing another cheer from those in the American ranks.

"Forward!"

Hour after hour the Battle of Palo Alto continued, with Taylor anticipating each Mexican move before it could be made. The Americans pushed the Mexicans back until, by nightfall, they occupied the positions from which the enemy had begun their attack that afternoon. Medical treatment was administered to the wounded, with American losses standing at nine dead and 45 wounded or missing. By comparison, Mexican losses were 200 dead and 300 wounded.

By morning, Taylor found that the enemy was still on the American side of the Rio Grande. They had, however, retreated to a far better defensive position, an old river bed called Resaca de la Palma. Because brush and thickets provided the Mexicans with numerous hiding places, some aides cautioned Taylor about engaging in further encounters in a territory that was so advantageous to the enemy. But not wanting to give the Mexicans an opportunity to regroup, the stubborn American commander gave his order: "Forward!"

Slowly, inch by inch, the American troops moved forward, many of them engaging in hand-to-hand combat with the Mexicans. The sound of exploding cannons and rifles blended with the voices of some men shouting directives and rallying spirits while others were pleading for their very lives.

Taylor ordered Captain Charles May to take his dragoons and capture the Mexican cannons. It was a wise decision. May's troops charged ahead on horseback, broke through the defensive lines, and quickly silenced the Mexican artillery. Not only did Captain May fulfill Taylor's command, he also captured General Diaz de la Vega, the Mexican field commander.

Confused and defeated, the enemy forces turned and ran, leaving some 500 of their comrades on the Resaca de la Palma battleground. Many more of the Mexican soldiers were lost as they tried to swim back across the Rio Grande to safety. Officially, Taylor gave credit for the victory to the "superior quality" of the American officers and men. But those who fought at Palo Alto and Resaca de la Palma knew that the real reason they won was due to the superb military leadership of "Old Rough and Ready."

A Happy Surprise

News of Taylor's victories against the Mexicans delighted all Americans and shocked some of them. Most people knew that the enemy greatly outnumbered the Americans. Because of this, there were many who had grumbled at the decision to put in command of the American troops a man who had never been to West Point, looked more like a farmer than a general, and was 60 years old! But the complaints stopped when news of Taylor's daring and resourcefulness spread across the country. Taylor's promotion to major general was assured and swift.

But Zachary Taylor had no desire to waste time. There was more work to be done. After a quick trip to Port Isabel to coordinate land strategy with naval operations, Taylor returned to his camp on the Rio Grande with plans to capture Matamoros.

Anticipating Taylor's actions, the Mexicans offered a truce, with the provision that the Americans stay out of Mexican territory, specifically Matamoros. Taylor would have none of it. Instead, he gave General Arista and men only two hours to leave the city. Although Arista did not respond to the ultimatum, Taylor did not start across the river two hours later. This was because sentinels reported signs of a Mexican exodus. If the town could be taken peacefully, so be it.

On May 18, 1846, that is exactly what happened as Taylor's troops rode toward Matamoros. After crossing the Rio Grande about two miles upriver from the town, they were met by civilian leaders. Without a shot being fired, Matamoros was turned over to the Americans. Taylor ordered no looting or plundering, just a peaceful and orderly occupation of the town.

Making Decisions

Sending a detachment of men to follow the fleeing Arista and his troops, Taylor faced a major decision—whether or not to pursue the Mexicans and engage them in combat. Scouts reported abandoned cannons and other military equipment. Surely the Mexicans would be easy targets. Taylor knew, however, that many Mexican soldiers would fight to the death, taking many Americans with them. He therefore turned a deaf ear to those officers who encouraged him to attack. It was a wise decision because the retreating Mexican soldiers became starving, half-crazed animals when they tried to cross a blazing desert with little food or water.

The waves of new recruits that poured southward seeking glorious military excitement proved to be another battle for Taylor to fight. Most of the new soldiers were untrained militiamen, poorly equipped for active battle and totally undisciplined. By the thousands they came, much more eager to soak up whiskey than take orders from their commanding officers.

To deal with the influx of new soldiers, Taylor established a system of military training for even the rawest of recruits. The system provided an extensive program of battle preparation in the briefest possible time.

Also appearing on the scene was Colonel Jefferson Davis, the man who had married Taylor's daughter Sarah. Davis was the leader of the First Mississippi Rifles, a volunteer regiment of horsemen. Because the regiment was well trained and the men were excellent marksmen, this contributed to a growing friendship between Taylor and his son-in-law.

In addition to the problems with all the new recruits, Taylor was also having communication problems with General Winfield Scott, the commander of the American forces in Mexico but seldom at the scene of action. President Polk finally grew weary of the confused orders being issued by "Old Fuss and Feathers" and removed him from his command, replacing him with Zachary Taylor.

TAYLOR FOR PRESIDENT?

In June of 1846, news of a different sort made its way to the military camp of General Zachary Taylor. A group of prominent American men had met in Trenton, New Jersey, to do some political planning. Unhappy with some of the recent occupants of the White House, the group wondered if Zachary Taylor might not be a good presidential candidate. Everyone remembered the leadership of George Washington and Andrew Jackson, both on the field of battle and as President of the United States. (Sadly, another former general, William Henry Harrison, had died within a month of becoming President, before his political leadership could be tried.) Was Zachary Taylor of the same quality? He seemed to be. Although not the most handsome and dashing in appearance, Taylor had proven himself to be an excellent military leader. He was respected by his troops and was a hero in the hearts and minds of his countrymen. Maybe he would consider being a presidential candidate if the opportunity should present itself.

When he heard this news, Taylor would have no part of such discussions. He was a soldier, a man doing his duty. If a presidential nomination came his way, from whatever political party or non-partisan group, he would decline. As soon as this war was over, Zachary Taylor was ready to hand in his resignation. He had no desire to go into politics.

There were also people in Washington who had different thoughts about Zachary Taylor's future. One was President James Knox Polk, who did not want to serve a second term. Nevertheless, Polk planned to play a key role in selecting the next presidential candidate for the Democratic Party. He knew the hero of the Mexican campaigns would bear careful watching. However, although Zachary Taylor had displayed few political inclinations, he clearly leaned more to the Whig philosophy than to that of the Democrats.

General Taylor took his time plotting the attack on Monterrey, using the Mexican military stronghold as an instructional lesson for his supporting officers. (Library of Congress.)

THE BATTLE OF MONTERREY

In the meantime, Taylor grew more and more impatient in Matamoros. Three-month volunteers came, were trained, and went back to their homes only to be replaced by more green recruits. At times, Washington seemed to have forgotten the ongoing war. Weeks slipped by without the necessary wagons and boats Taylor had ordered so that he could make his next move – to capture Monterrey.

Monterrey was the most important city in northern Mexico. It was located some 250 miles southwest of Matamoros, in the valley of the San Juan River. The western approach to the city was protected by a fort called Bishop's Palace, while the eastern approach was protected by two forts, Diablo and Teneria. In front of Monterrey was a fortress called The Citadel. All of these outposts would be heavily fortified with guns and men.

Actually, each building in Monterrey was its own fort, constructed of thick adobe walls and stone roofs. Because of its strategic location, the city controlled the best route from the Gulf Coast plains to the Mexican highlands, and, ultimately, to Mexico City. It was clearly the next logical target for Taylor and his troops.

Time to Move

Taylor had requested wagons to carry supplies over the land route. He had also requested steamboats to carry troops up the Rio Grande to where it joined with the San Juan River, and then into Monterrey.

But the wagons and steamboats did not come. Exasperated with the delay, Taylor finally ordered 300 soldiers to proceed some 60 miles west to the Mexican town of Reynosa. This mission was accomplished without a fight. Then, with the arrival of some boats in July, additional troops were dispatched to Carmargo, three miles from the Rio Grande-San Juan River junction. When the requested wagons still had not arrived by August, Taylor decided he could not wait any longer. He assembled a force of 6,000 men, about half the soldiers he had hoped to take, leaving behind the most untrained and undisciplined volunteers.

There were some American officers who thought that Monterrey might be taken without a fight. There was so little Mexican resistance during the last few battles that even Taylor himself hoped that perhaps a bloody encounter could be avoided. But the Mexicans had no intention of giving up Monterrey without a fight.

General Pedro de Ampudia commanded 7,300 of the finest Mexican troops and knew the value of his strategic location. Taylor, too, knew that if the Mexicans chose to fight, he would have to make the most effective use of his troops,

who were outnumbered by over 1,000 men. He assigned Brigadier General William Worth to Bishop's Palace on the west,
while Lieutenant John Garland was directed to engage the
Mexican forces at Diablo and Teneria. He would personally
command the frontal attack on The Citadel. Learning that
General Santa Anna was heading north with Mexican reinforcements, Taylor knew his mission had to be accomplished
as quickly as possible.

The Fight for Monterrey

The fighting began on September 19 with a rainstorm of cannon and rifle fire drenching the American forces. Though
somewhat outnumbered, the better discipline and training of
the American troops quickly became evident. Within two days
Worth had taken Bishop's Palace, and Garland captured Diablo and Teneria.

Taylor concentrated on the most dangerous and difficult
goal, storming The Citadel, overpowering the Mexican
brigades there, and chasing the routed enemy out into the city.
Although each building in the fortress housed soldiers with
guns, Taylor led the way, constantly exposing himself as a
target yet never being hit. "I don't think he'd tell any of us
if he *were* shot," one American artilleryman told a cluster
of his comrades.

On September 24, five days after the battle began,
General de Ampudia knew there was no point in continuing
the fight. With a group of his top aides, he rode to Taylor's
tent and offered to surrender. Taylor accepted, but generously
allowed the remainder of the Mexican Army to leave the city.
Taylor also agreed to give de Ampudia and his men an eight-
week head start before pursuing them.

The grace period was a kind act, to say the least, considering that the United States and Mexico were officially at

The defending Mexicans could not stop the onslaught of attacking American troops as they fought their way into the main plaza during the Battle of Monterrey on September 23, 1846. (Library of Congress.)

war. But Taylor knew his own men were tired, supplies were low, and it would be virtually impossible to feed and guard thousands of Mexican prisoners. De Ampudia gratefully accepted the terms of surrender and immediately prepared to vacate the city of Monterrey.

Angry Reaction in Washington

When news of Taylor's actions reached Washington, President Polk was furious. There already was criticism that the war against Mexico had gone on too long, and the Whig Party was gaining more and more positive attention with each passing day. Polk publicly criticized Taylor for allowing the Mexican soldiers to go free. He claimed that Taylor was "no doubt brave" and willing to fight, but that his leadership was indeed open to question.

Learning of Polk's remarks, Taylor merely shrugged. "Maybe our distinguished President would like to come down here and do a better job himself," the general grumbled. But beneath the surface, Taylor was seething. He never acted without careful consideration and he knew his military tactics were correct in the given situation. To expedite the war, Polk reinstated General Winfield Scott as commander of the Mexican Expeditionary Forces. "Old Fuss and Feathers" had high praise for Taylor's actions in capturing Monterrey, but the terms of capitulation, he said, were reprehensible. Scott claimed that Taylor's actions had come close to bringing about a recall of the general, but that "his standing with the public alone saved him."

There was no question about that. The general public feasted upon news of American victories in Mexico, and Zachary Taylor was given much of the credit. Letters written by soldiers in the service continued to bolster his image, and newspaper editors began to hint openly that Taylor displayed all the characteristics of a President. Even young children joined in the admiration, chanting a crude rhyme:

> Old Zach's at Monterrey,
> Bring out your Santa Anner;
> For every time we raise a gun,
> Down goes a Mexicanner.

As the people, young and old, relished and retold the stories about Taylor, President Polk became all the more determined to prevent a future presidential bid by the hero of the Mexican campaign. Compounding Polk's problem was the fact that the Whigs also had another military hero, General Winfield Scott, in their corner as a candidate.

An Intercepted Letter

As for Taylor, he became anxious to rejoin the fighting rather than sit out the rest of the campaign. Scott, however, preferred that Taylor remain at Monterrey while his troops were sent on various missions. Then came news that a messenger carrying a letter from Scott to Taylor had been ambushed by the Mexicans. In the letter, Scott had spelled out the complete U.S. strategy, including planned attack dates, estimated numbers of troops, supply routes, and other data for the remainder of the military campaign. In the hands of Mexican leader Santa Anna, the letter was reading at its very best!

While Santa Anna enjoyed reading the intercepted correspondence, Taylor perused communication of a different sort. In the off-year election for the House of Representatives, the Whigs had taken a definite majority over the Democrats, 117 to 110. Clearly the American people had wearied of Democrat Polk and his treatment of the Whig generals, especially Taylor. Should the nomination for President be offered him in the next election, Zachary Taylor made up his mind to accept it. He would show those people in Washington a thing or two.

PLANNING A TRAP

But there was a war to win first. With each passing day, Taylor became more and more frustrated. He led his troops into small Mexican towns, such as Saltillo and Victoria, barely encountering any opposition. Then would come orders commanding Taylor to send detachments of his troops elsewhere. While lesser officers were leading bigger brigades, Taylor was merely biding his time.

The last straw came when Scott wrote Taylor and told him to "abandon Saltillo and make no detachments, except for reconnaisances and immediate defense much beyond Monterrey." Accepting Scott's communication as only a suggestion, Taylor immediately led his troops 17 miles south to Hacienda Agua Nueva. There, he hoped to lure Santa Anna, the Mexican leader, into a fatal trap.

Using all his knowledge of and experience in military tactics, Taylor prepared for Santa Anna. He established a frontal position at Hacienda Agua Nueva and a back-up position at Hacienda Buena Vista. Actually, more attention was focused on the Buena Vista location because any attacking force would have to go through a narrow passage before reaching the flattened plateau on which Hacienda Buena Vista was located.

Santa Anna could not resist the temptation. His scouts and spies informed him that Taylor's soldiers numbered less than 5,000 while the Mexican leader had assembled an army of 20,000. Surely capturing or killing Major General Zachary Taylor would be the most effective way to turn the entire war around. After wiping out the Americans in the north, he could take his Mexican forces to Veracruz, which the Americans planned to invade from the sea. Yes, going after Taylor was a worthy plan.

"Let the Mexicans Come"

Once news of Santa Anna's movements reached Taylor, the old soldier was delighted. "Let the Mexicans come," he exclaimed, "and damned if they don't go back a good deal faster than they came." He reviewed plans with his officers, checked on supplies, inspected the troops, and made certain everything was in readiness.

Santa Anna's troops had to cross 300 miles of desert. They marched at an exhausting pace while the leader himself sat in a golden coach pulled by eight white mules. The sun beat down heavy and hot, draining the strength from the men. As they drew near to Agua Nueva, the spirit of the men heightened. They were eager to do battle. But when they discovered the outpost in ashes, already destroyed, the morale of the Mexican soldiers plummeted.

Convinced that Taylor was already retreating and not planning or desiring a direct encounter, Santa Anna moved toward Buena Vista. On the morning of February 22, 1847, Santa Anna's troops arrived at the Buena Vista passage. A few Mexican cavalrymen moved forward under a sign of truce to deliver a message to Taylor. Santa Anna urged the American leader to surrender, to avoid "a catastrophe." The Mexican general gave his American counterpart an hour to make up his mind.

No hour was needed. "General Taylor never surrenders!" the stern commander snapped. "Santa Anna can go to hell!"

The couriers argued further, trying to persuade Taylor to give up. The conversation went nowhere. As the cavalrymen returned to Santa Anna, American gun crews readied their cannons.

The Battle of Buena Vista

Santa Anna was in no hurry. Slowly he made final plans for the attack. Learning that his supply position at Saltillo was in danger, Taylor led a troop of soldiers there, not wanting anything to happen that would endanger his overall plan. By the time he returned to Buena Vista the next day, fighting had already commenced.

From the very first shot, the Americans began to pull back, seemingly overwhelmed by the large number of approaching Mexican soldiers. "Into the fight!" Taylor commanded, sitting high on Old Whitey. "Into the fight!" His men glanced at their leader, rallied by his spirit, and collected their courage. Sideways on his horse Taylor sat, in full view of all his troops – and the Mexicans. Foolish? Perhaps. But daring enough to raise the fighting spirit of his men. A Mexican rifleman took aim and sent a bullet ripping through the sleeve of Taylor's coat. He did not look down. Another shot tore a button from the front of his chest. Taylor sat still, shouting out orders, steadying his horse. He swept the battleground with his binoculars. "Give them a little more grape, Bragg," he hollered to Captain Braxton Bragg, who eagerly loaded more cannons with grapeshot, spraying the enemy with deadly force.

At a strategic moment, Taylor gave the order for Colonel Jefferson Davis and his Mississippi Rifles to charge. Though injured, Davis led his troops in a V formation, trapping Mexican cavalrymen inside. Where sabers failed, the Mississippians showed their skill with bowie knives and combat on the ground.

In the meantime, Mexicans were attempting to capture the American supply position at Saltillo. But the soldiers Taylor had stationed there would not give way, fighting with the same spirit as the men at Buena Vista.

By nightfall, neither side could claim victory. Both forces had suffered serious losses. But in the rays of morning sunlight came a strange yet welcomed sight – the Mexican troops were gone. Their ability to continue fighting effectively had been almost totally destroyed. It was a satisfied Zachary Taylor who rode Old Whitey around the blood-stained battlefield that day, satisfied that his plans had been so successful. But there were no smiles, no joy in his victory. Too many Americans had been killed or wounded.

A NATION'S HERO

It was a month before news of Taylor's victory at Buena Vista reached President Polk and the rest of the nation. "Why, the man was outnumbered three to one!" some declared. "I heard four to one!" others argued. But there was no argument regarding how the people felt about Major General Zachary Taylor. He was a hero, with few men his equal.

There was little joy in the White House, however. President Polk shook his head in disgust and disbelief over a general who ignored orders, entered battles that should never have been fought, much less won, and emerged as a modern-day George Washington. To Polk, who had a far better understanding of the political world than the military, Taylor's actions were motivated by his desire to become President.

Despite Taylor's heroism and personal appeal for the people, Polk refused to permit any special honors be given the military leader. He spent the rest of the war doing very little, while Scott led the final American victories at Veracruz and Mexico City.

But a new door was opening for Zachary Taylor – opening to a life that was entirely different from anything he had ever done before. Yet, as he had in the past, he would still continue serving his country.

Chapter 9

"Old Rough and Ready"

By the autumn of 1847 it was clear that it was only a matter of time before the Mexican Army would be totally crushed and the war would be over. It was equally clear that the powers that be were going to keep Zachary Taylor in northern Mexico killing time rather than enemy soldiers. Therefore, he asked for a six-month leave, hoping to return to his plantation at Cypress Grove, which he had longed to enjoy for many years.

When his leave was approved in November, the tired old general set sail for New Orleans. Because the ship was filled beyond capacity with wounded soldiers returning home, Taylor insisted on giving up the quarters reserved for dignitaries. Instead, he slept on a mattress in the boiler room. "There's less noise from people passing," he joked.

If Taylor had expected to return home without notice, he was in for a major surprise. As his ship entered New Orleans harbor, it was met by boats with cheering crews and clanging bells, causing the usually serious Taylor to break into a happy smile. His joy was further increased by the sight of his wife, Peggy, waiting on the dock, for they had not seen each other for the last two years. Daughter Betty was there, too, her face reflecting the love of a daughter and the pride of a nation. Yes, Zachary Taylor was glad to be home.

TO RUN – OR NOT TO RUN?

But before all the homecoming festivities had ended, there were new decisions to make – decisions that could not be put aside. Because 1848 was a presidential election year, newspaper reporters and businessmen were constantly asking Zachary Taylor if he was going to run for President. A few years before, he would have laughed aloud at the very idea. Run for President? What a preposterous idea! Why, he had never stayed in one place long enough to even be eligible to vote for a President. But as he heard with increasing frequency that Winfield Scott might obtain the Whig nomination in 1848, Taylor became more intrigued by the idea.

As he became aware of the increasing number of people who seemed to want him to be a candidate, and the intensity with which they expressed themselves, Taylor began giving the matter additional thought. His personal feelings about Polk were a further incentive, for he could imagine no greater joy than sharing with his nemesis a coachride to a presidential inauguration.

Not that Taylor felt confident that he would get the nomination and be elected. Some of the northern Whig leaders had little use for a presidential candidate who owned slaves. Although Taylor insisted that those slaves who worked on his plantation at Cypress Grove were well treated, the fact that he owned some 150 of them made him one of the major slaveowners in the entire nation.

Other Whigs pointed to Taylor's lack of political experience. Running a country was not at all like running an army, and Taylor had few valid credentials that would equip him for the former responsibility. Furthermore, why choose an exhausted general like Zachary Taylor when there was a statesman like Senator Henry Clay who was available? Clay had been the Whig presidential candidate in 1844 and lost. But times were different now. President Polk had lost much of the nation's support, and it appeared that whoever the Whigs nominated had a good chance for victory.

The Pressure Mounts

As 1848 began, more and more people were encouraging Taylor to state once and for all whether or not he would be a candidate for the presidency. Henry Clay was particularly insistent, hoping that Taylor might step aside and endorse him, as did General Winfield Scott. But until the war with Mexico was over, Taylor still had his military responsibilities and could not appear to be actively pursuing a political career.

Taylor refused to declare anything at all. Instead, he spent most of his days at the Baton Rouge cottage, tending to Peggy, who was ill much of the time, and posing for artists and sculptors who had come to make a likeness of "America's greatest living hero." Although lacking any formal political experience, it was obvious that Taylor had an innate sense of the right thing to do to maintain interest in him as a candidate.

Not only the Whigs, who knew that Taylor had very little understanding of their political philosophy, but other political groups considered him a major contender. Yet he refused to adopt any partisan stands. "If I be a candidate, it shall be as a candidate of the people, not a party," he declared.

However, Taylor knew that to be elected he had to have a knowledge and an awareness of what was going on in the nation. To quiet some of the opposition concerning his ownership of slaves, Taylor stated his support of the Ordinance of 1787, a law limiting slavery from spreading into the west and southwest. Many of his southern slaveowner friends resented

Taylor's stand, but he paid no attention to them. Northern leaders, however, respected him for speaking out.

Nor did Taylor remain silent about maintaining a strong peacetime Army—it was imperative, he said. He also advocated higher tariffs to bring in the revenue needed to pay for it. Taylor also felt that it was essential to reduce government operating costs, and that the sale of public lands could bring in funds for reducing the national debt.

A series of letters that Taylor sent to his brother-in-law carried additional policy statements that made their way into the press:

> The personal opinion of the individual who may happen to occupy the executive chair ought not to control Congress upon questions of Domestic policy; nor ought his opinions & objections to be interposed when questions of Constitutional power have been settled by the various Departments of government and acquiesced by the people.

In his directness and honesty, Taylor attracted both slaveowners and abolitionists (those opposed to slavery). One southern slaveowner feared that, once in office, Taylor might cause him to lose his 100 slaves. Always candid, Taylor responded that he himself now owned some 300 slaves!

Cass Leads Democrats

In May of 1848, the Democrats met in Baltimore, Maryland, and nominated Lewis Cass of Michigan to carry their party banner in the race for the presidency. Taylor noted with interest that one of his aides, General William Butler, was chosen to run for Vice-President. But it was not a unified convention. Many of the Democrats, particularly those who felt the antislavery platform was too weak, threatened to break away from the party in the fall.

The Choice Is Made

Two weeks later, the Whigs held their convention in Philadelphia. As voting opened for the presidential nomination, Taylor led the pack with 111 of the 279 possible votes. Clay came in second with 96, while Scott collected 43. On the second ballot, Clay's strength slipped by 11 votes, while both Taylor and Scott added to theirs. As lesser candidates dropped out of the race, Taylor increased his lead in the third ballot to where he was only eight votes short for the nomination.

Afraid that some compromise candidate might be put up, the leaders of the Taylor campaign announced to the convention that their candidate would support whoever the Whigs nominate. It seemed a noble gesture on Taylor's part because there were a number of splinter political groups that might back Taylor if the Whig convention chose someone else. Noble or not, it was a shrewd political ploy, and Taylor carried the nomination on the fourth ballot. Millard Fillmore of New York was picked to run with him for Vice-President.

A BITTER CONTEST

The 1848 presidential campaign became rather nasty quite early. Taylor saw nothing wrong with accepting the support of any coalition offering it. When southern Democrats and Independents meeting in Charleston gave him their backing, he happily accepted, much to the consternation of Whig leaders in New York. "But they are also backing Henry Dodge for Vice-President, not Millard Fillmore!" they protested. But Taylor would not listen. Nor would he speak out more definitely on the slavery issue, whereas Cass advocated "squatter sovereignty"–that is, the residents of the territory or state in question should settle the issue.

Planting Seeds

"For too long women have been mere ser-
vants to men. It is time we stood up for our-
selves and demanded that which is rightfully
ours."

The words were those of Elizabeth Cady
Stanton as she stood before the women attending a convention held in Seneca Falls,
New York. The year was 1848, the same
year the Whig Party met in Philadelphia to
nominate General Zachary Taylor as their
presidential candidate.

There were those, especially of the male
gender, who were quick to sneer and jeer at
the revolutionary outbursts of Elizabeth Cady
Stanton. "Probably some jilted old maid!"
more than one man was heard to grumble.
Stanton's remarks had no such origin. The
daughter of a lawyer, Elizabeth grew up hearing her father offer advice and counsel to
women who lived in a society that denied
them the right to vote, own property, or even
share guardianship of their own children.

If unhappy, women were wise to complain
quietly, as most states had statutes that per-
mitted wife-beating. Although she married
and bore seven children, Elizabeth Cady Stanton picked up the gauntlet on behalf of all
women.

At the Seneca Falls conclave in 1848, cru-
sader Stanton opened the proceedings with
an impassioned "Declaration of Sentiments,"
18 points of grievance directed at men. In
format and style, the grievances were pat-

terned after the Declaration of Independence, with "men" and "he" substituted for George III. Stanton's own document began: "We hold these truths to be self-evident: that all men and women are created equal."

Stanton pulled no punches as she lambasted the domination of men over women. "He has compelled her to submit to laws, in the formation of which she had no vote. He has withheld from her rights which are given to the most ignorant and degraded men—both natives and foreigners. He has taken from her all right in property, even to the wages she earns." On and on went the litany of abuses, eloquently written and condemning in their content.

Lucretia Mott, an ally of Stanton's and a mother of six, cautioned against seeking the right to vote, but Stanton would not back down. "Women's suffrage [the right to vote] is a necessity if we are to ever achieve equality," she insisted, and the Seneca Falls gathering wholeheartedly endorsed the "Declaration of Sentiments."

One conferee at the Seneca Falls meeting left with new passion for the women's cause. Within months, Amelia Jenks Bloomer was publishing *The Lily,* a periodical devoted to championing women's right to higher education, to vote, and to fair marriage laws. She attracted large audiences (and controversy as well) dressed in full trousers, a short skirt, and a tight bodice. The trousers became known as "bloomers," in honor of the crusading feminist. "But listen to my words, don't just notice what I'm wearing!" Bloomer demanded. "As women fighting for a cause, we must expect physical and mental punishment, but we have been taking that treatment for years."

Bloomer's prediction was accurate indeed. Leaders of the women's movement were subjected to stone-throwing and spitting, while name-calling and verbal attacks caused the fainthearted to back away. Taylor and those who immediately followed him in the presidency paid little attention to those speaking out in behalf of the "weaker sex," but seeds had been planted that would bring a rich harvest of rights for women in the generations that followed. Once told by men to "go home and take care of their husbands and homes," women like Stanton, Mott, and Bloomer today enjoy a revered place of honor by all those who accept the belief "that all men *and* women are created equal."

Mudslinging was rampant in the months before the election. Taylor was frequently depicted by the Democrats as a stingy, nearly illiterate farmer who would ruin the stability of the national government, just as he had destroyed his plantation land. Few pointed out, however, that Cypress Grove fell victim to frequent flooding. Taylor, nonetheless, kept the place going largely to help the slaves it supported.

Cass, on the other hand, was accused by the Whigs of underhanded dealing while he was an Indian agent in the

A campaign poster showing the Whig ticket of Zachary Taylor and Millard Fillmore that was victorious in the 1848 election. (Library of Congress.)

Northwest. They claimed he had accumulated a sizable fortune through a number of questionable business transactions.

Those foolish enough to ridicule Taylor's military service during the War of 1812 found themselves laughed at loudly. For if there was anything that all people agreed upon during the campaign, it was Taylor's achievements in military service. Not many remembered the War of 1812 in any detail, but there was no forgetting the role that "Old Rough and Ready" had played during the war with Mexico.

Counting the Votes

The Election Law of 1845, which marked the beginning of the electoral college, became effective with the presidential election of 1848. There was little doubt that Taylor's chances of winning were greatly improved by the fact that former President Martin Van Buren ran on a third-party ticket, the Free Soil Party. A disgruntled Democrat who could not abide Cass' soft stand on the slavery issue, Van Buren did not get one electoral vote. However, he managed to take enough popular votes away from Cass that Taylor was able to poll 163 electoral votes to Cass' 127.

Taylor took the news of his victory clamly, even "solemnly" observed one newspaper reporter. Undoubtedly, there were many thoughts on his mind. After 40 years of military service, that phase of his life was ending. It was being replaced by a task that he felt little prepared to assume.

Taylor's beloved Peggy made no secret of her unhappiness at having to leave their comfortable home in Baton Rouge for "that big white barn in Washington." Thankfully, their daughter, Betty, who was to be married in December, agreed to act as Taylor's hostess in the White House. Her husband-to-be, William Wallace Bliss, graciously consented.

At age 64, Zachary Taylor was about to become the 12th President of the United States. He hoped and prayed he was equal to the task.

Chapter 10
New Duties

Following his election victory, President-elect Zachary Taylor visited a clothesmaker in Baton Rouge in order to purchase two new suits. "Don't think those Washington folks would appreciate my usual soldiering garb," he told friends, "and I don't want them to think me any more a skunk farmer than some of them already think me to be."

When he returned to pick up the finished outfits, the clothesmaker gave Taylor a handful of cards and messages. "They're from people who have requests for jobs," he explained. "Did they give you money to pass them along?" Taylor asked. Nodding affirmatively, the clothesmaker looked down. "Nothing for you to be ashamed about," the old general insisted, as he dropped the cards and messages in the nearest wastebasket. "I respect an enterprising young fellow like yourself, but I have little use for those who pay for special favors."

PICKING HELPERS

In January of 1849, Zachary Taylor resigned from the United States Army. He then bid his friends and neighbors in Baton Rouge a sad goodbye and headed for Washington. Upon his arrival in the nation's capital, Taylor spent the time before his inauguration in March attempting to put together a Cabinet. Unfortunately, not all of his choices were available. His

Zachary Taylor took his oath of office as the 12th President of the United States in the east portico of the U.S. Senate on March 5, 1849. (Library of Congress.)

longtime friend, Senator John Crittenden from Kentucky, wished instead to serve as the state's next governor. It was a big disappointment to Taylor, who had hoped that Crittenden would be willing to serve as his secretary of state.

Certainly the senior statesmen of the Whig Party, Daniel Webster and Henry Clay, were out of consideration for Cabinet posts. Upon learning of Taylor's nomination by the Whigs, Webster had let loose a tirade against "that swearing, whisky-drinking fighting frontier colonel," and it was rumored that he still felt the same way.

Clay, though not given to open tantrums, felt betrayed by his party for not nominating him, and he wanted no part of any Taylor administration. Moreover, while the Battle of Buena Vista in Mexico may have propelled Zachary Taylor to the presidency, it had also claimed the life of Henry Clay, Jr., a loss that his father still felt deeply.

Without Webster and Clay, Taylor would be deprived of some of his party's best talent. He would have to rely on many second choices as well as on the advice of Whig Party officials.

On March 5, 1849, Zachary Taylor accompanied outgoing President James Knox Polk to the official inauguration ceremonies at the east portico of the Senate. Roger B. Taney, Chief Justice of the U.S. Supreme Court, would administer the oath of office making Zachary Taylor the 12th President of the United States.

Many of the 20,000 people who had gathered for the event were interested in what the new President would have to say about his future plans for the nation. However, in one of the shortest inaugural messages of any incoming President, Taylor failed to specifically identify any programs he would innovate. The speech was more of a welcoming address, sharing a few personal convictions. He promised to rely on his Cabinet for help, as well as on the lessons provided by "illustrious patriots" of the past, particularly George Washington.

Taylor noted that he agreed heartily with Washington's policies of staying free of entangling alliances, preferring instead a strict neutrality. As to the slavery controversy, Taylor stated, "I will look with confidence to the enlightened patriotism of Congress to adopt such measures of conciliation as may harmonize conflicting interests, and then to perpetuate the Union, which should be the paramount object of our hopes and affections."

Party Problems

In the days and weeks that followed Taylor's inauguration, the White House was filled with Whig leaders and underlings. Relying heavily on the advice of party leaders, Taylor selected the members of his Cabinet, most of whom were virtual strangers to him. Naturally, all were Whigs. Newspaper editors had mixed evaluations of Taylor's Cabinet choices. Their opinions ranged from "the weakest bunch in many years" to "respected and able men, every one of them." Taylor hoped the latter was closer to the truth because he knew he would be relying heavily on his administrative team.

The absence of Whig leaders Webster and Clay from Taylor's Cabinet was noted by political observers from the very beginning as evidence of in-fighting among members of the party. Furthermore, just among the New York group, Vice-President Millard Fillmore had his own following, as did Senator William Seward and Thurlow Weed, a newspaper editor from Albany. Other Whig leaders also controlled factions, and each wanted a voice in dispensing political jobs. Although Taylor emphasized the need to pick people based on their honesty and ability to perform, a pledge he had made during his inaugural address, few politicians listened to him.

MEETING THE PUBLIC

But from the very beginning, Zachary Taylor was willing to listen to others – too willing, some of his aides thought. He welcomed into the White House anyone who wanted to talk to him. After seating his guest, he would prop his feet up on his desk and listen. Occasionally, he would eject a stream of tobacco juice toward a cuspidor on the floor near the door, seldom missing. Taylor's white shirts often bore proof of his spitting habit, which he had acquired during his years as a soldier. However, female guests saw no such displays of behavior. They left meetings with the President remarking as to his good manners and kind conduct.

Tobacco spitting was not the only remnant of his military days that Taylor brought to the White House. His faithful horse, Old Whitey, received the best of attention in the nearby stables and also enjoyed the greenest and fullest patches of grass available on the White House lawn. Whenever Taylor needed to escape the taxing pressures of the presidency, he would have Old Whitey saddled up and take a brisk ride around the city. More than once Taylor might have wished that he was again chasing Seminoles in Florida or a troop of Mexican soldiers outside of Matamoros. How simple those conflicts seemed compared to the complicated problems in Washington.

AN UNUSUAL SECRETARY

The person most likely to send Taylor riding for having created domestic or international problems was Secretary of State John Clayton. There was no doubt that Clayton was a brilliant lawyer, capable of using the smallest detail to its maximum effect. And his eloquence with the English language was hardly surpassed by anyone in Washington ("He can breathe life into the deadest tariff bill," Taylor once observed).

No one was more impressed with these strengths than Clayton himself. Aides reported that he would become virtually enraptured debating with himself in an empty room, frequently pausing to exclaim over his own flowery oratory. But overblessed as he may have been with intellect and the power to use words, Clayton lacked manners and diplomacy in dealing with other individuals. Those doing business with the secretary of state would often leave his office both impressed and insulted.

Clayton wasted no time in offending French Ambassador William Tell Poussin, who had filed a claim against the United States for the destruction of French property during the Mexican-American War. By any diplomatic standards, it was a trivial matter, but Clayton disliked Poussin's attitude and said so publicly. This was a reprehensible breach of decorum, offending not only Poussin personally but the French people generally. When he learned of the situation, Taylor might have taken action and resolved it to everyone's satisfaction. However, because his inexperience provided no guidance in such matters, he preferred to let his Cabinet members attend to their own problems.

Relations with France became even more strained after an American ship, the *Iris,* pulled a French vessel, the *Eugenie,* off of a reef near Veracruz when the latter ran aground. It was thought to be an act of courtesy exchanged by ships on the high seas until the captain of the *Iris,* Edward Carpenter, submitted a claim requesting payment for salvage.

French Ambassador Poussin, still smarting from the earlier incident with Clayton, was furious. To avoid any further international problems, Poussin was recalled to France. But then the new American ambassador to France was directly snubbed by French Foreign Minister Alexis de Tocqueville. Clearly, the French expected a formal public apology, if not from President Taylor, at least from his secretary of state. Either action would have resolved the matter, but Whig advisors encouraged Taylor to stay quiet, to remain firm. However, French President Louis Napoleon smoothed the matter over by receiving the American ambassador himself, thereby avoiding any further tension. It was too trivial a concern to risk annoying Taylor and the American Congress.

THE CLAYTON–BULWER TREATY

Each time Secretary of State Clayton seemed to have made a mountain out of a molehill through some diplomatic error, he would immediately redeem himself by some clever act of shrewd manipulation. The Clayton-Bulwer Treaty was one of those acts which showed that John Clayton was more than an amateur statesman in the realm of international diplomacy.

In addition to Taylor's election as President in 1848, other major events of that year included the discovery of gold in California and the signing of the Treaty of Guadalupe Hidalgo. The treaty ended the Mexican-American War and gave the United States some 500,000 square miles of land. People eager to "strike it rich" were heading west to search for gold or to settle on the new land.

However, the land journey was long and dangerous, as was the route by sea around Cape Horn. To make the trip faster and safer, Commodore Cornelius Vanderbilt proposed a canal route across Nicaragua. (Panama would have been more advantageous, but Vanderbilt's competitors already had control of that possibility.) Because no American investors would back his idea, Vanderbilt sought financial help in England.

Having already recognized the value of such a waterway, the English government hoped to build a canal itself and retain complete control over it. When President Taylor heard of this possibility, he would have none of it. "No European nation shall operate such a waterway in the western hemisphere," he insisted. "A canal of this nature should be independently operated for the benefit of all nations."

For a time, it was a battle of "one upsmanship," with both the United States and England making separate treaties with parties in the area involved. As more and more information leaked out to the general public about the controversy, English citizens claimed their country's right to proceed with plans for a canal. Taylor, however, remained adamantly against any foreign meddling in the American hemisphere.

What finally emerged from meetings and discussions between England and the United States was the Clayton-Bulwer Treaty, named in recognition of Secretary of State Clayton and British Minister Henry Bulwer. The treaty provided for freedom of movement through any canal built in Central America while denying dominant influence to either the United States or England. Naturally, the agreement failed to satisfy those Americans who had hoped the United States would enhance its international prestige by building a canal to link the Atlantic and Pacific Oceans. But the agreement not only ended any possibility of British expansion in Latin America, it also paved the way for the eventual construction of the all-important Panama Canal.

MILITARY ADVENTURES

Just as President Taylor would not be pressured into asserting American power over its southern neighbors in order to expand the nation, he was equally against doing so in other directions. Shortly after taking over the presidency, British officials expressed concern over those who hoped to make Canada a part of the United States. When Taylor learned that private American troops were being assembled for this purpose, he threatened to send federal regiments northward to put down any such military adventures.

He issued the same warning upon hearing that men were being recruited for military duty in Cuba, in hopes of forcing annexation of that country to the United States. "No Americans shall actively participate in armed expeditions against friendly nations," Taylor declared, "in that such participation will be considered a violation of the neutrality laws of the United States."

For a man who had spent 40 years actively engaged in his country's military service, President Zachary Taylor appeared to be trying to avoid any possible military confrontation at all costs. Nonetheless, he was forceful and firm in his handling of international matters.

Taylor also refused to allow the country to be used for military purposes by other nations. President Polk had authorized use of the Brooklyn Naval Yard for converting an American vessel into a German fighting ship. Germany was then at war with Denmark and wanted the ship for military purposes. Taylor, however, stopped the program, citing the neutrality policy of the nation. He insisted that Germany first had to guarantee not to use the vessel against any country at peace with the United States. Not wishing to risk its friendly relationships with America, Germany agreed.

SLAVERY–THE MAJOR ISSUE

There was one major issue that transcended all others during the 16 months of Taylor's administration. In homes across the country, Americans discussed and argued the issue of slavery. It was talked about on every possible level – moral, economic, social, and political. The topic was discussed even more heatedly in Washington, where southern lawmakers strongly supported slavery while northerners opposed the entire concept.

Most southerners felt confident that President Taylor, one of the largest slaveowners in the nation, would extend slavery into the newly acquired territories of California and New Mexico. But in August of 1849, Taylor surprised many northerners and southerners alike when he publicly announced that "the people of the North [need] have no apprehension of the further extension of slavery." By suggesting that the people of both territories apply for statehood and then be allowed to write their own constitutions, Taylor was almost welcoming them into the Union as free states.

Naturally, southerners felt that the President had betrayed them – that he had become "a Southern man with Northern principles" and was providing the opportunity for free states to dominate slave states. Perhaps, some of the southern leaders thought, their President did not understand the depth of their feelings. Therefore, a representative group of southerners called upon Taylor at the White House to present their case.

At the mere suggestion that continued support of free states might cause some southern states to leave the Union, the President's eyes sparked with rage. In no uncertain terms, he informed his visitors that if, in carrying out the laws of the United States, it would become necessary for him to personally take command of the Army, he would do just that. Furthermore, he would hang those in rebellion against the Union with less reluctance than he had hung deserters and spies in Mexico! "The Union must be preserved," he insisted, "and upon its preservation must depend our own happiness and that of countless generations to come. Whatever dangers may threaten it, I stand by it."

Taylor's position did little to soothe the tempers of either northern or southern legislators in Washington. When words got too hot, fists took over, even among those who would have been thought too old for such behavior. "It is a pathetic sight to find that in the nation's capital, those men sent to share thoughts and to reason collectively choose to act like animals of mere instinct," wrote one newspaper editor. "Let us hope and pray that The Father of Our Country is not watching his children during these times."

State of the Union Address

From his State of the Union message to Congress on December 4, 1849, Washington lawmakers hoped to draw some definite sense of direction of how Taylor planned to handle the slavery issue. Granted, he had been in office only for nine months, but he had showed boldness and force in his handling of international squabbles. "I don't often agree with the man," observed Daniel Webster, "but he *does* make decisions." Others agreed, and even those southerners who felt betrayed by a fellow southerner still hoped for some form of reconciliation.

The speech was a disappointment. Not that Taylor failed to give suggestions in many areas of governing. He provided an eloquent plea on behalf of economic enterprise within the nation, calling for duties on imported products so that domestic commodities could receive protection. He called for an agricultural bureau in the Department of the Interior, "to elevate the social condition of the agriculturalist, to increase his prosperity, and to extend his means of usefulness to his country, by multiplying his sources of information." A transcontinental railroad was suggested, with a recognition of the country's westward expansion and its need to coordinate land and waterways for the benefit of the nation's present and future citizens.

On the issue of slavery, however, Taylor offered no progressive thoughts, no directives, no challenging theories of resolution. There was only a warning to anyone who might disrupt the Union that he held dear, his delivery clearly reflecting his inexperience with formal speaking:

> For more than half a century, during which kingdoms and empires have fallen, this Union has stood unshaken. The patriots who formed it have long since descended to the grave; yet still it remains, the proudest monument to their memory and the object of affection and admiration with everyone worthy to bear the American name. In my judgment its dissolution would be the greatest of calamities, and to avert that should be the study of every American. Upon its preservation must depend our own happiness and that of countless generations to come. Whatever dangers may threaten it, I shall stand by it and maintain it in its integrity to the full extent of the obligations imposed and the powers conferred upon me by the Constitution.

Eloquent words they were, given with reverence if not professional projection. Yet, there was no answer concerning the slavery issue in Taylor's message. For that, the lawmakers had to turn to themselves.

The following month, Taylor returned to Congress, this time delivering one speech to the senators and another to the members of the House of Representatives. The message, one they had heard before, was the same to each: The people of California and New Mexico should be allowed to determine their own status "upon the principles laid down in our own Declaration of Independence."

The Compromise of 1850

The national lawmakers turned to themselves to resolve the question of free and slave states. Henry Clay chaired a group called the Committee of Thirteen, consisting of six Democrats and seven Whigs. Their task was to prepare a legislative document concerning the determination of free and slave states that would be acceptable to both North and South. That document, called the Compromise of 1850, included legislation that would admit California as a free state, admit Utah and New Mexico as uncommitted territories, require the capture and return of runaway slaves by all states and territories, and prohibit slavery in the District of Columbia.

Taylor had little use for compromise of any kind. And within this particular legislation, he even found parts that were unconstitutional. Again and again he read the sections, each time finding new weaknesses and areas that would cause dissension among different parts of the country. Clearly, "Clay's Compromise" was trying to do too much, to please too many and yet not pleasing anyone at all. Surely slavery could be better resolved. But how?

Then, as so often happens, in the midst of one trouble came another. For President Zachary Taylor, a scandal within his administration temporarily interrupted the slavery problem.

Chapter 11

Scandal!

It had all started some 75 years before, 10 years before Zachary Taylor was born, during the times when America was struggling for its own existence. The Creek and Cherokee Indians had received $50,000 worth of goods in exchange for certain territorial lands. Now, in 1850, descendants of the Indians claimed the entire transaction had been mismanaged, if not illegal, and that the United States government owed them $191,352 in accumulated interest. This was a considerable amount, as the entire national debt at the time was only $16 million.

Although he had served as attorney of record for the Indians claiming the reimbursement, Attorney General Reverdy Johnson, a Taylor appointee, approved the claim and sent it on to another Taylor appointee, Secretary of War George Crawford. If Crawford had inspected the claim closely, he would have noticed the conflict of interest in Johnson's roles. Instead he paid little attention to it, passing it on to one more Taylor appointee, Secretary of the Treasury William Meredith, who immediately authorized payment of the entire amount. The transaction, known as the Galphin Claim, attracted little attention at the time, but it was soon to mushroom into a major scandal. It was a matter of particular agony for Taylor because he knew nothing about the Galphin Claim and had never been consulted as it moved toward settlement.

THE SCANDAL BREAKS

Taylor's ignorance of the transaction made no difference to those congressmen who were opposed to the President for one reason or another, felt betrayed by his lack of support for fellow southerners, or simply wished to grab public attention. As the story unraveled, eyebrows were raised when Johnson's role as attorney for the claimants was revealed. Then, when Secretary of War Crawford was declared to be one of the beneficiaries of the claim, people started asking questions. Were these the same men President Taylor had declared to be "harmonious, honorable, patriotic, talented, hard-working and of irreproachable private character"? How hollow his words sounded, in the shadow of their actions.

At the worst, the Galphin Claim seemed to be an organized conspiracy by a few highly placed individuals to defraud the government. At the least, those involved reflected stupidity and incompetence. Whatever their motivation or intention, one fact remained clear—all were appointments of the man in the White House, President Zachary Taylor. This was the same man who had pledged "careful spending by the government in order to build a strong and solvent nation."

ACCEPTING THE BLAME

Despite the fact that Taylor had made his Cabinet selections largely on the recommendations of Whig Party leaders, he was not about to shift the responsibility and blame for the Galphin Claim scandal to anyone else. After all, the men involved were *his* men, part of his presidential team. Throughout his military career, Taylor had always assumed responsibility for lesser officers he had sent to fulfill his commands. He saw this as being a similar situation as far as accountability was concerned.

Agonizing over the problem, the President reached out to Thurlow Weed, an early political friend and advisor, for guidance. "I'd like to throw out the lot of them," Taylor moaned. "I have had nothing but complaints about this department or that secretary. Now this. Would it not be the best course to dismiss the whole damn bunch?"

Weed shook his head and argued that to do so would not clear the air as Taylor hoped. Instead, it would appear that Taylor had indeed picked nothing but incompetents upon entering office. Anyway, who would he get as replacements?

Taylor hedged, suggesting those innocent of any questionable conduct could be given diplomatic jobs after dismissal, but the bad apples would be thrown out. Time would soothe the situation, Weed promised, and suggested that no action be taken at the present time.

CAUSE FOR CONCERN

When he left the White House, Weed was not only concerned with the gravity of the Galphin Claim scandal, he was even more troubled by President Taylor's appearance. Never had he looked so drawn and haggard. What *was* the condition of Taylor's health? After all, it was only June of 1850, and there were almost three years remaining in his term. Weed wrote a letter to Taylor's son-in-law, Major William Bliss, expressing his personal concern. In return, Bliss promised to look into the matter as soon as possible.

It was virtually impossible to turn away from the problems of the day, but Taylor tried. The rides on Old Whitey offered some moments of relaxation, as did morning walks on the White House grounds. Gardeners soon learned to be on their best behavior at all times, not knowing when the President might come strolling by.

Although Peggy still would not perform any official hostessing duties, she had gotten in the habit of inviting close friends in for private visits, and even occasionally joining these guests at their homes for family dinner parties. There is little doubt that Taylor shared the agony of his office to some extent with his wife, but there was little that she could offer in terms of practical advice and direction. Surely there were times when both of them longed for the peace and comfort of the small cottage back at Baton Rouge. Perhaps someday . . .

In the meantime, there were affairs of the moment to deal with. Taylor pledged himself to maintain the Union at whatever cost necessary. No, there would be no breaking away, no separate northern and southern states—the states would be united, pure and simple. Whatever compromises, alliances, or arrangements Congress might devise, the United States of America would continue to live, to grow, to remain strong.

Chapter 12
Final Taps

The debate over slavery raged as hot and furious as the summer air in Washington in 1850. Everywhere people debated the strengths and weaknesses of the Clay Compromise. But news of President Zachary Taylor's illness after attending the Fourth of July festivities at the Washington Monument brought a lowering of voice and deep personal concern. Even among his enemies and opponents, Taylor was respected.

Those who might assail his aptitude in office, or lack of it, would not deny his past heroic exploits on the field of battle. "President Zachary Taylor lies ill in the nation's capital this night," wrote one newspaper editor, "and although we have criticized his actions while in office, we pray for his recovery. With or without a rifle, this man is a quality soldier and a hero of this nation."

It was a sentiment felt by Americans everywhere. In hushed but proud tones, old soldiers shared stories of fighting with "Old Rough and Ready" in the War of 1812, in Florida against the Seminoles, and in Mexico at Buena Vista. "He loaned me his sleeping bag once," boasted one fellow. "Said he could sleep on hard ground with or without. He was snorin' in two minutes." "Always liked his whiskey," shared another former soldier, "but never did see him drunk. Didn't believe in such things."

Hours slipped into days as family and friends kept vigil over the sick President. Dr. Wood, his son-in-law, arrived to offer support to both the medical staff and the family. Only Peggy seemed to think there were signs of improvement, remarking that he had "been in worse shape with the fever more than once." But her face could not hide her concern.

THE END NEARS

On July 8 Taylor shared a few thoughts with an attending male nurse. "I did not expect to encounter what has come to me in this office," the weakened President offered. "God knows I have tried to do my honest duty. But I have made mistakes, my motives have been misconstrued, and my feelings have been outraged." They were sad, angry statements by a man who felt betrayed.

By the next day it was apparent that the end was near. Debate over slavery raged on the Senate floor, but when Daniel Webster rose to announce, "A great misfortune threatens this nation. The President of the United States is dying, and may not survive the day," there was silence. Quietly the senators adjourned. In the House of Representatives, members received the news with saddened faces. If anyone could contain the southerners, it was Zachary Taylor. With him gone, no one knew what would happen.

That evening carriages rolled slowly up to the White House to deposit those who had come to wait out the final hours. With the leader's family stood his former son-in-law, Jefferson Davis, who Taylor had once assailed for marrying his daughter Sarah but who now had become a close friend. Vice-President Millard Fillmore was there, hardly a close ally but ready to take over the duties of the presidency. Members of the Cabinet joined Fillmore, their voices low and subdued.

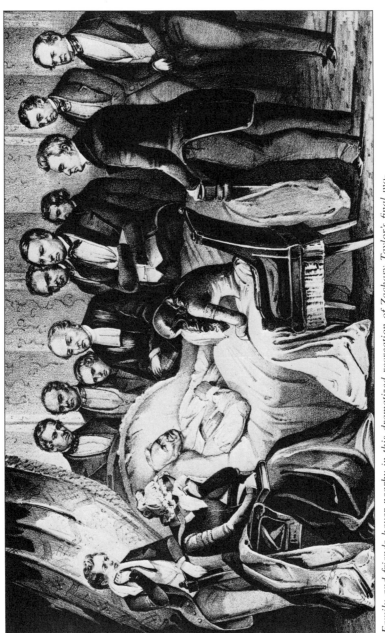

Family and friends hover nearby in this dramatized recreation of Zachary Taylor's final moments. He died on July 9, 1850. (Library of Congress.)

A SOLDIER DIES

Shortly after ten o'clock, Taylor lifted himself to speak. His words were slow but clear. "I am about to die," he said. "I expect the summons very soon. I have tried to discharge my duties faithfully; I regret nothing, but I am sorry that I am about to leave my friends." Slowly the weakened man lay back, his breathing heavier. In a few moments, he was dead.

Washington church bells tolled out the sad news. Members of the House of Representatives gathered to hear Abraham Lincoln, a Whig from Illinois who had fought with Taylor in the Black Hawk Wars, rise to extol the fallen leader's virtues. In the Senate, it was the venerable Daniel Webster who took the floor and acclaimed "the noble and brave Zachary Taylor."

General Winfield Scott led the funeral procession on a spirited horse, while Taylor's faithful Old Whitey, his saddle empty and his master's boots turned backward in the stirrups, followed the funeral wagon. Thousands lined the Washington streets on that day, July 13, as the body of Zachary Taylor was temporarily laid to rest in the Congressional Cemetery on the Potomac River. In the fall, the body was taken to lie forever in the family cemetery on Beargrass Creek in Springfield, Kentucky.

That same year, the Compromise of 1850 was passed by Congress. "If Taylor had lived, he would have vetoed this legislation," noted Daniel Webster. "We would likely have had a civil war." For that, the country would wait another 10 years. The new President, Millard Fillmore, did something no other Vice-President had ever done upon succeeding to the presidency—he accepted the resignations of all government department heads and appointed an entirely new Cabinet. "Old Rough and Ready would have liked that!" noted the old sage Webster.

THE TAYLOR LEGACY

George Washington did his country a major disservice. While that statement sounds blasphemous, it is, nonetheless, true. By providing exemplary leadership on the battlefield during the Revolutionary War, he won the love and respect of his countrymen. By a similar display of quality performance as the first President of the United States, Washington solidified the reputation he had achieved as as wartime general. However, in fulfilling both roles so well, he made Americans think that there was a direct relationship between a person's ability to lead troops in war and his ability to lead a nation. History has proven that this is not necessarily true.

One of Washington's greatest talents was his ability to pick the right men for the right jobs. During the Revolutionary War, he managed to draw the best out of men like Nathaniel Greene, Henry Knox, Anthony Wayne, even, for a time, Benedict Arnold. As President, he continued his ability to choose wisely, surrounding himself with such men as John Jay, Thomas Jefferson, Alexander Hamilton, and again, Henry Knox. John Adams, as Washington's Vice President, also provided excellent leadership.

Although Zachary Taylor made his entry into politics over 50 years after Washington had exited as President, Americans still hoped that a good general would also make a good President. After all, Andrew Jackson, like Washington, had first been a general, then President. Having also served in the U.S. Senate, Jackson understood politics and left an impressive mark on American history. Because William Henry Harrison, who also had first been a general, died after a month in office, he did not have a chance to fulfill what many thought would have been a triumphant administration. (Harrison understood politics, too, having served in the U.S. House of Representatives.) Enter Zachary Taylor, battleworn from some 40 years in military service. Although he had no political experience whatsoever, much was expected of him.

TAYLOR APPRAISED

Unfortunately, Taylor was not destined to live long enough to fulfill even a single term of office. His death after only 16 months in the presidency offers historians only a brief glimpse of his performance as the country's chief executive. In few categories does he achieve any standard of "greatness" or "excellence." In handling international affairs, Taylor was forceful and firm. He was not afraid to act decisively, but he cautiously avoided any confrontation that might bring about war. He stood solidly behind a declaration of neutrality, working to keep the United States free of foreign entanglements.

Taylor's first and only State of the Union Address, delivered in December of 1849, shows a keen awareness of domestic needs. He supported domestic businesses, with raised tariffs if necessary to protect American products. He also advocated a Department of Agriculture and an improved transportation program for the nation.

As for resolution of the slavery issue, however, Taylor could offer no innovative program. He alienated his fellow southerners by advocating California's admission to the Union as a free state, and expressed hope that New Mexico would do the same. It seemed hypocritical that slaveowner Taylor would embrace the philosophy of northerners toward slaves, but it was merely his unstinting desire to keep the Union intact.

Although Taylor personally had no responsibility in the Galphin Claim scandal, the entire affair tainted the honor of his administration. Over-reliance on advice offered by Whig Party leaders contributed to the selection of Cabinet members who left something to be desired. Yet, because he had never been involved in politics, Taylor had no way of knowing firsthand the men he was choosing to help him lead the country. Nevertheless, although Taylor was shabbily treated, he must still assume responsibility for his subordinates.

The legacy of Zachary Taylor is that of a good military leader, a general who knew how to wage war effectively and to get the most out of his men. He never lost a battle and enjoyed the respect of his troops, leading them to nickname him "Old Rough and Ready."

As President, Taylor displayed some qualities of executive leadership in his handling of international affairs and in the programs he advocated for domestic business, agriculture, and transportation. However, the solution of the slavery issue was beyond his grasp; it remained for a civil war to be fought before it was resolved.

Bibliography

Bailey, Thomas A. *The Pugnacious Presidents.* New York: The Free Press, 1980. A brief but penetrating look at Zachary Taylor's handling of potentially explosive situations during his 16 months as President of the United States.

Bassett, Margaret. *American Presidents and Their Wives.* Freeport, Maine: Bond Wheelwright, 1969. Peggy Smith Taylor gets more than "equal time" in this collective biography of those men who occupied the White House and their wives. The spotlight is on character traits and personality, rather than mere chronological facts and figures.

Coit, Margaret L. *The Sweep Westward.* Alexandria, Virginia: Time-Life Books, 1963. This book is particularly useful in its coverage of the southwestern war campaigns from 1829 to 1849, in which Taylor played so important a role.

Hamilton, Holman. *Zachary Taylor, Soldier of the Republic.* Indianapolis: Bobbs-Merrill, 1941. A well-written account of the life of the 12th President of the United States. With drama and accuracy, Hamilton brings Taylor to life.

Hoyt, Edwin P. *Zachary Taylor.* Chicago: Reilly & Lee, 1966. Hoyt specializes in writing biographies about Americans who played important historical roles but are almost forgotten. This book offers not only a look at Zachary Taylor the man, but also the country and events around him.

Kent, Zachary. *Zachary Taylor*. Chicago: Children's Press, 1988. Kent's offering of Taylor is one of the Encyclopedia of Presidents selections, a photo-filled, easy-to-read series. Of special interest are the various journal and diary entries scattered throughout the text, recorded by those who lived through the events covered.

Morgan, James. *Our Presidents*. New York: Macmillan, 1924. This collection of capsule biographies offers essential facts about each President in a unique and personal writing style typical of the times in which it first appeared.

Whitney, David C. *The American Presidents*. Garden City, New York: Doubleday, 1978. In simple, straight-forward style, Whitney traces the background and road to the White House of each chief executive. The results upon arrival provide for excitement and drama, even in the case of Taylor's brief occupancy.

Wilkie, Katharine E. *Zack Taylor: Young Rough and Ready*. Indianapolis: Bobbs Merrill, 1952. The spotlight is on youth in this highly fictionalized but fast-moving story about Zachary Taylor as a boy. The facts may be altered for the sake of drama, but the character ingredients remain intact.

Williams, T. Harry. *The Union Sundered*. Alexandria, Virginia: Time-Life Books, 1963. This volume in the Time-Life Series covers the period 1849–1865. Opening with Taylor's climb to the presidency, the book gives readers a clear understanding of the America he so briefly led.

Young, Bob and Jan. *Old Rough and Ready*. New York: Messner, 1970. The publisher is famed for its stable of factual, dramatic biographies, and this volume is no exception. Not only is the reader given an accurate portrayal of Taylor's life, from start to finish, the authors penetrate the surface of the man to analyze many of his motivations.

Index